1 MONTH OF FREE READING

at

www.ForgottenBooks.com

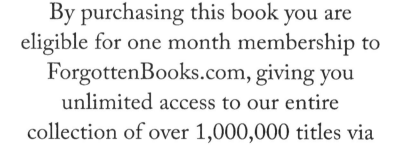

By purchasing this book you are eligible for one month membership to ForgottenBooks.com, giving you unlimited access to our entire collection of over 1,000,000 titles via our web site and mobile apps.

To claim your free month visit:
www.forgottenbooks.com/free910054

* Offer is valid for 45 days from date of purchase. Terms and conditions apply.

ISBN 978-0-265-92111-1
PIBN 10910054

This book is a reproduction of an important historical work. Forgotten Books uses state-of-the-art technology to digitally reconstruct the work, preserving the original format whilst repairing imperfections present in the aged copy. In rare cases, an imperfection in the original, such as a blemish or missing page, may be replicated in our edition. We do, however, repair the vast majority of imperfections successfully; any imperfections that remain are intentionally left to preserve the state of such historical works.

Forgotten Books is a registered trademark of FB &c Ltd.
Copyright © 2018 FB &c Ltd.
FB &c Ltd, Dalton House, 60 Windsor Avenue, London, SW19 2RR.
Company number 08720141. Registered in England and Wales.

For support please visit www.forgottenbooks.com

Newspaper postage only is chargeable on this sheet.

Terms:—Weekly, $2; Semi-monthly, $1; Monthly, 50 cents. NEW-YORK, FEBRUARY, 1848. Subscriptions invariably in advance.

REMOVAL.
TWEEDY & BARROWS,
Wholesale Dealers in
Fancy and Staple
DRY GOODS,
YANKEE NOTIONS, &c. &c.
Have **REMOVED** from 58 Broad-st., to
No. 80 CEDAR STREET,
[NEAR BROADWAY.]

The subscribers, grateful for the very liberal patronage bestowed upon them in past years, would respectfully announce to their customers, and purchasers of **DRY GOODS** generally, that they have made arrangements to add to their former general Stock, a VERY EXTENSIVE ASSORTMENT of **DOMESTIC GOODS**, (which are offered for CASH,)

Consisting, in part, of

Brown & Bleached Sheetings & Shirtings.	Cotton Yarn.
Do do Drillings.	Cotton Twine.
Bed Ticks.	Cotton Wick.
Shirting Stripes.	Cotton Wadding.

COTTON BATTS, &c., &c.

A call is respectfully solicited from your House, when you visit the city, before making your purchases elsewhere, feeling confident that it will be for your advantage to examine our Stock.

TWEEDY & BARROWS,
80 Cedar-street, near Broadway.

UNITED STATES.

Treasury Notes, 6 per cents, — 1 to 1¼ dis.
Do. do. mill & five 2-5ths, — do
500 dollar Treasury Notes, altered from the Eagle Mining Co. of Indiana; vignette a stooping eagle on the limb of a tree, Washington on the left end, and the goddess of Commerce on the right. Very unlike the genuine.

MAINE.

Agricultural Bank, Brewer, — Broke

Audroscoggin Bank, Topsham, — ¼
[Chas. Thompson, Pres., John Coburn, Cash.]

Augusta Bank, Augusta, — do
[Thos. W. Smith, Pres., George W. Allen, Cash.]
1's, let. E; good imitation—pay M. Crady, Jan. 1, 1842. Perkins' old steel plate.
1's, **2**'s & **5**'s, altered from some broken bank.
3's, lett. A., Jan. 1842, stereotype plate.

Bangor Commercial Bank, — Closed

Bank of Bangor, Bangor, — ¼
[Samuel Veazie, Pres., W. S. Dennet, Cash.]
☞ Beware of bills which read "Bangor Bank."
1's, **2**'s, **3**'s and **5**'s, altered; hold them to the light.

Bank of Cumberland, Portland, — do
[Wm. Moulton, Pres., Samuel Small, Cash.]
3's, let. B vig. a ship and Mercury—steamboat between the officers names. Paper very poor.
5's, vig. a ship under full sail; the head of Jackson on the right end, and Van Buren on the left—well done.

Bank of Old Town, Orono, — Fraud
Bank of Portland, Portland, — Closed

Bank of Westbrook, Westbrook, — 3
[S. Jordan, Pres., A. G. Fobes, Cash.]

Bath Bank, — Closed

Belfast Bank, Belfast, — ¼
[James White Pres., N. H. Bradbury, Cash.]
☞ Beware of drafts of the LUMBER ASSOCIATION on this bank, dated in New-York City.

Brunswick Bank, Brunswick, — do
[Richd. T. Dunlap, Pres., A. C. Robbins, Cash.]
3's. This bank has redeemed all its genuine 3's.

Calais Bank, Calais, — 10
[G. Downes, Pres., J. A. Lee, Cash.]

Canal Bank, Portland, — ¼
[J. B. Osgood, Pres., J. B. Scott, Cash.]
1's, altered from a broken bank—Heward, cash.
2's, altered from a broken bank, Heward, cash.
20's, altered from a broken bank—hold it to the light.
50's, altered from a broken bank. "CANAL" and "Portland" slightly defective; signatures poorly done.

Casco Bank, Portland, — do
[Eliphalet Greeley, Pres., John Chute, Cash.]
2's, altered from the broken Citiz. Bk. Augusta.
5's, altered from some fraudulent institution.

Castine Bank, — Broke
Central Bank, Hallowell, — ¼
Citizens' Bank, Augusta. — Fraud

Commercial Bank, Bath, — ¼
[J. Robinson, Pres., Thos. Agry, Cash.]
2s, let. A, vig. rail cars and laborers, a man on horse and a man with a scythe. Altered from a Michigan Bank.
2s, **3**s, **5**s & **10**s, altered from a Michigan bank.
10s, altered, vig. cog-wheels, vessel, and rail cars in the distance. "Bath" and "Maine" are defective.

Damariscotta Bank, Noblebor, — Closed

Eastern Bank, Bangor, — ¼
[A. M. Roberts, Pres., W. H. Mills, Cash.]
☞ beware of drafts of the N. Y. Foreign and Domestic Exchange Co. payable at this bank.
1's, counterfeit, let. D—badly done.
3's, let. A., May 4, 1838. The fine print is defective.
5's, altered from the Globe Bank of Bangor, Howard, cash., Parsons, pres., and some have Bryant, pres.

Exchange Bank, Portland, — Closing

Franklin Bank, Gardiner, — ¼
[Henry Bowman, Pres., Hiram Stevens, Cash.]

Frankfort Bank, — Broke

Freemen's Bank, Augusta, — ¼
[Benj. Davis, Pres., Wm. Caldwell, Cash.]
3's, **5**'s & **10**'s, altered from broken Citizens' Bank; likely to deceive. Paper is whiter than the genuine.

Frontier Bank, Eastport, — do
[Samuel Wheeler, Pres., Edward Ilsley, Cash.]
1's & **5**'s, altered—Frontier and Eastport badly put on.

Gardiner Bank, Gardiner, — do
[Sam. C. Grant, Pres., Joseph Adams, Cash.]
2's, let. A.—blurred, particularly the ends and "two."
3's, let. A. various dates, Sam'l C. Grant, pres., Joseph Adams, cash. The bills appear blurred.

Georgia Lumber Co., Portland, (D.) —
Globe Bank, Bangor, — Fraud

Granite Bank, Augusta, — ¼
[Wm. Woart, Pres., Silas Leonard, Cash.]
5's, altered from broken Citizens Bank, Augusta, Me.

Hallowell and Augusta Bank, — Broke

Kenduskeag Bank, Bangor, — ¼
[G. W. Pickering, Pres., T. J. Dodd, Cash.]
5's, let. L. pay H. Clay, June 18, 1832.
5's, let. L. pay C. Carroll, Sep. 1832, T. S. Dodd, cash., & Wilkins, pres. Parts of the bill are pale, others dark.

Kennebec Bank, — Broke
Kennebunk Bank, — Closed

Lime Rock Bank, Thomaston, — ¼
[Knott Crockett, Pres., E. M. Perry, Cash.]

Lafayette Bank, Bangor, — Closed

Lincoln Bank, Bath, — ¼
[Geo. F. Patten, Pres., John Shaw, Cash.]
5's, let. L. "patent five" round the letter.

Manufacturers' Bank, Saco, — do
[Wm. P. Haines, Pres., S. S. Fairfield, Cash.]
10's, an alteration; description not known.

Maine (late Cumberland) **Bank,** — Closed

Manuf. and Traders' Bank, Portland, — ¼
[J. Richardson, Pres., E. Gould, Cash.]

Mariners' Bank, Wiscasset, — do
[Henry Clark, Pres., S. P. Baker, Cash.]

Medomac Bank, Waldoborough, — do
[James Hovey, Pres., Geo. Allen, Cash.]
3's, an alteration; vig. two females and anchor

Megunticook Bank, Camden, — ¼
[Joseph Jones, Pres., Hiram Bass, Cash.]
3's, altered from the broken Citizens Bank of Augusta, Me.

Mercantile Bank, Bangor, — 5

Merchants' Bank, Portland, — ¼
[Wm. Woodbury, Pres., R. Mitchell, Cash.]
1's, let. A. June 6, 1839, H. Ellis. cash. B. Brant, pres. Engravers. Terry, Pelton & Co., Boston and Prov.
5s, vig. a female, grain, sickle, &c.; a female on each end. Has Durand & Co. N. Y., as engravers. Poor imitation.
5s, vig. a female with a sickle and sheaf of grain, man on a horse in distance; goddess of Liberty on left end.

Northern Bank, Hallowell, — ¼
[F. Glazier, Pres., J. C. Dwight, Cash.]

Neguemkeng Bank, — Closed
Oxford Bank, Fryeburgh, — Fraud
People's Bank, Bangor, — Closed
Passamaquoddy Bank, — Broke

Sagadahock Bank, Bath, — ¼
[Joseph Sewall, Pres., D. F. Baker, Cash.]

Saco Bank, — Closed
St. Croix Bank, Calais, — Closed

Skowhegan Bank, Bloomfield, — ¼
[Wm. Allen, Pres., S. Philbrick, Cash.]
10's, an alteration; counterfeit signatures.

South Berwick Bank, South Berwick, — do
[W. A. Hayes, Pres., Chas. E. Norton, Cash.]

Still Water Canal Bank, — Broke

Thomaston Bank, Thomaston, — ¼
[Richd. Robinson, Pres., J. D. Barnard, Cash.]
5s, vig. Mercury, shipping, &c.
5s, the red—"Thomaston Bank" and "Maine" blurred—engraved by N. Eng. Bank Note Co. Well done.

Ticonic Bank, Waterville, — ¼
[Timo'y. Routtelle, Pres., Augus. Perkins, Cash.]

Union Bank, Brunswick, — Closed
☞ The time for redeeming its notes expired June 1, 1845.

Waldo Bank, Belfast, — Closed
Washington Co. Bank, Calais, — Closed
Waterville Bank, — Broke
Winthrop Bank, — Broke
Wiscasset Bank, — Broke

York Bank, Saco, — ¼
[Jona. King, Pres., Henry S. Thacher, Cash.]
5's, purporting to be Perkins' stereotype plate—those having a check plate on the back, have not been counterfeited.
5's, let. L, pay F. Lord, May 6, 1832, Henry S. Thatcher, cash. Jona. King, pres. Dark impression.

NEW-HAMPSHIRE.

Ashuelot Bank, Keene, — ¼
[Sam'l Dinsmoor, Pres., T. H. Leverett, Cash.]

Bank of Lebanon, Lebanon, — do
[Robert Kimball, Pres., J. H. Kendrick, Cash.]
2s, let. A; S in Hampshire is not on a line with the rest.
2's and **3**'s, counterfeit.
20's, vig. a farmer seated with sickle. End pieces, steamboat and rail cars. Engraved by Boston Bank Note Co. Also, **5**'s, **10**'s and **50**'s.

Belknap County Bank, Meredith,............ ¼
[Warren Lovell, Pres., J. T. Collin, Cash.]

Cheshire Bank, Keene, (New,)................ do
[John Elliot, Pres., J. H. Williams, Cash.]
☞ The genuine bills of the old Bank are redeemed at the new institution.
10s, lithograph—vig. a large X with portraits each side; the vig. and heads each side are miserably engraved.

Claremont Bank, Claremont,..................Closed

Concord Bank, Concord,.........................Closed

Commercial Bank, Portsmouth........(Closed) ¼

Connecticut River Bank, Charlestown,.. .... do
[John W. Tappan, Pres., Geo. Olcott, Cash.]
5's let. B; A. G. Brown, pres., P. Butler, cash. "Charlestown" and "New-Hampshire" are stamped in.
5's & 10's, altered—vig. a stream of water and saw mills on each side. E. P. Butler, cash.
50s, altered from 3s; goddess of Liberty on the right end with coat of arms of Mass. on a shield; on the left an agricultural scene—sheep shearing at the bottom.

Derry Bank, Derry,........................... do
[A. Tucker, Pres., Jas. Thom. Cash.]
2's, let A; appears blurred, particularly the ends.
2's, Nov. 2, 1842; the words "two" and "New Hampshire," badly done. Pay to J. Jay.

Dover Bank, Dover,.............................. do
[J. H. Smith, Pres., Andrew Pierce, Cash.]
☞ The charter of this Bank having expired, it has ceased operations, except to wind up its concerns.
5's, let. A, Jona. Dame cash., A. Peirce, pres. Well done.

Exeter Bank, Exeter,.............................Closed

Farmers' Bank, Amherst,........................Closed

Granite Bank, Exeter,........................ ¼
[James Bell, Pres., James Brownley, Cash.]
5's, altered from broken Citiz. B., Augusta, Me.
5's, vig. a steam ship—a female with a sickle. Paper white and thick, engraving coarse.

Grafton Bk, (late Coos,) Haverhill,..............Closed

Great Falls Bank, Somersworth,............... ¼
[D. H. Buffum, Cash.]

Hillsboro' Bank,...................................Broke

Lancaster Bank, Lancaster,.................. ¼
[Royal Joyslin, Pres., Geo. A. Cossitt, Cash.]
5's, let. A., an alteration; A. Phelps, Cash., Samuel Root, Pres. Others, Geo. Young, and A. Parker.

Manchester Bank, Manchester,............... do
[Jas. U. Parker, Pres., Nathan Parker, Cash.]
3's, let. B. vig. a ship and Mercury—steamboat between the officers' names. Paper very poor.
5's, vig. cattle, &c., engraved by Toppan, Carpenter & Co. N.Y. Two 5s on left end, a head and a female on the right.
5's, let. A. vig. a group of cattle—Nathan Parker, cash, J. W. Parker, pres. —Oct. 3, 1845.

Manufacturers' Bank, New-Ipswich,......... do
[Jonas M. Melville, Pres., Geo. Barrett, Cash.]
2's, Perkins' stereotype plate—genu. of this plate all in.

Mechanics' Bank, Concord,..................... do
[J. M. Harper, Pres., Geo. Minot, Cash.]
5's, altered, vig. a man ploughing; a large 5 on each side.
10's, plate is different from the genuine, and coarse.

Mechanics' & Traders' Bank, Portsmouth,.. do
Late Commercial.
[Richard Jenness, Pres., Jas. F. Shores, Cash.]

Merrimac County Bank, Concord,............ do
[Matthew Harvey, Pres., E. S. Towle, Cash.]
5's & 10's, altered from Stillwater, worthless, vig. saw mills and stream of water—Butler, cash.

Nashua Bank, Nashua, ... do
[Isaac Spalding, Pres., John M. Hunt, Cash.]
5's, "o" in No at the top of the bill is omitted; has "FIVE" on the left hand corner, genuine has "V," and is ¼ of an inch shorter than the genuine.

New-Hampshire Bank, Portsmouth,..........Closed

New-Hampshire Union Bank, Portsmouth,.Closed
5's, let. J. old plate, coarsely engraved. Signatures of Pres. and Cash. same handwriting.

Piscataqua Exchange Bank, Portsmouth,.. ¼
(*Formerly the "Piscataqua Bank."*)
[W. ILY. Hackett, Pres., Samuel Lord, Cash.]
2's, let A; plate of the old bank—appears blurred.

Pemigewasset Bank, Plymouth,.....(Closing) do

Portsmouth Bank, Portsmouth,......(Closing,) do
[R. Rice, Pres., J. M. Tredick, Cash.]

Rochester Bank, Rochester,..................... do
[Simon Chase, Pres., John M'Duffee, Cash.]

Rockingham Bank, Portsmouth,............... do
[J. M. Tredick, Pres., J. S. Pickering, Cash.]

Strafford Bank, Dover,......................... do
☞ Notes of the old bank dated previous to 1847 are redeemed by the new bank until July 1st, 1847.

Winnipisiogee Bank, Meredith,............ ¼
[Ebem Coe, Pres., John T. Coffin, Cash.]

Wolfborough Bank,.............................. 1
[D. Pickering, Pres., C. Rust, Cash.]
2s, coarse and indistinct—has a plain black margin on the left end, the genuine has a figure 2 in each corner.

VERMONT.

Agricultural Bank,..............................fraud

Bank of Burlington,........................ ¼
[E. T. Englesby, Pres., R. G. Cole, Cash.]
2's, let. B—Franklin on the left end; "TWO" on right, upper corner—genuine has "2" & die-work on the right end.
5's, the dies, in which are the figure 5's, on top of the bill, are circular,—in genuine are elliptical—coarsely engraved.

Bank of Black River, Proctorsville,......... do
[E. F. Parker, Pres., D. A. Heald, Cash.]

Bank of Brattleboro',......................... do
[E. Seymour, Pres., H. S. Noyes, Cash.]
2's, let. A. pay J. Frost, June, 1838. The counterfeit is spelt BRATTLEBOROUGH, the genuine BRATTLEBORO'.

Battenkill Bank, Manchester, Vt............ do
[Major Hawley, Pres't, Wm. P. Black, Cash.]

Bank of Orange County, Chelsea,........... do
[Lement Bacon, Pres., E. C. Redington, Cash.]
1's, let. E, Jan. 20, 1841, pay to E. D. Blodgett. Perkins' stereotype plate. Paper of a light texture.
2's, let. A, paper good; Steele, cash., Francis, pres.
2's & 3's, let. A. pay M. Colby, June 4, 1841, Jason Stote cash., John Francis, pres't.
3's, lett. A., Jan. 25, 1841 and 1842, pay E. Blodgett, John Francis, Pres., Jason Steele, Cash.
3's, lett. A., pay E. D. Blodgett, Oct. 20, 1841.
50s. altered from bills of a smaller denomination.

Bank of Caledonia, Danville,................. do
[Geo. B. Chandler, Pres., J. A. Page, Cash.]
2s, vig. a man on horseback, cattle, &c.; letter B.
3s, variously filled up, paper and engraving dark.

Bank of Manchester,.......................... do
[M. Brown, Pres., . Cash.]
3's, altered from 1s—look at "THREE DOLLARS."
5's, let. A. altered from 1's; red back. Vignette, a lady, with a sickle.
10's, altered from 2's; an X pasted over the figures on the ends, and "Ten" over the "Two," in the body of the bill.
50's, vig. a winged female, &c., engraved by Durand and Co.—Rawdon, Clark & Co., Albany, engraved the genuine.
100's, vignette a female holding a shield and flag, and an eagle—the bank has not issued 100's.

Bank of Middlebury,........................... do
[W. Nash, Pres., J. Warner, Cash.]
10's, vig. ship, railroad and agricultural view. No engraver's name.

Bank of Montpelier, Montpelier............... do
[T. Reed, Pres., George Howes, Cash.]
1's, let. E. pay C. W. S., May 4, 1841, D on each end
1's, counterfeit, same as the 3's that follow.
2's, paper & execution good; observe a blank space under "Bank of Montpelier,"—letter A.
3's, let. A., stereotype plate. "Payable at Suffolk Bank, Boston;" this is not on genuine bill.

Bank of Newbury, Wells River,................ do
[Timothy Shedd, Pres., O. C. Hale, Cash.]

Bank of Orleans, Irasburgh..................... do
[Ira H. Allen, Pres., George C. West, Cash.]

Bank of Poultney,.............................. do
[M. G. Langdon, Pres., M. Clark, Cash.]

Bank of Rutland,................................ do
[G. T. Hodges, Pres., W. Page, Cash.]
5's, altered from 2's. Hold them to the light.
5's, let. I. pay M. Strong or bearer, dated 23d May, 1825, W. Page, cash., R. Temple, pres.

Bank of St. Albans,............................. 1
[James Davis, Pres., A. Houghton, Cash.]
☞ Beware of bills of Mech. Exch. Co. on this bank—they read "pay for the Mechanics' Exchange Co., New-York."
2's, lett. I. dated 1st Jan. 1829, pay to A. Jones, A. Plimpton, Cash., B. Smith, Pres.
3's, let. A. pay to L. Sandford, Nov. 10, 1837; T. A. Walker, cash., W. R. James, pres. ST. ALBANS is are stamped on, before the date, in dark printed type.—poor imitation.

Bank of Vergennes, Vergennes,............... ¼
[F. Huntington, Pres., I. Scott, Cash.]
1's, pay to the bearer, J. Scott, cash. Wm. H. White pres.
3s, let. A, vig. rail cars; a ship on the right, and female on the left lower corner—dog and safe between the signatures.—Purports to be engraved by W. Dane & Co.
5's, altered from 1's. Easily detected.

Bank of Woodstock,................(closing) do
[Job Lyman, Pres., E. Johnson, Cash.]
3's, pay H. Hall, dated Oct. 10, 1827. Coarsely done, resembling lithography; on poor paper.
5's, let. A. engraved by Reed & Bessell, S. C., N. Y. A miserable imitation.
5's, let. A. pay A. Kent or bearer, June 5, 1840, R. Van Cott, pres., Jno. Billings, cash. Engraving coarse, paper light.

MASSACHUSETTS.

Bank of Windsor, ... Broke

Bellows Falls Bank, Rockingham, ... ¼
[N. Fullerton, Pres., Wm. Henry, Cash.]
5's, bill appears dark, paper thin, vig. coarse.

Bennington Bank, Bennington .... Broke
Commercial Bank, Poultney .... fraud
Essex Bank, Guildhall, ... Broke

Farmers' Bank, Orwell, ...
[A. L. Catlin, Pres., Wm. B. Martin, Cash.]
1's, let. B. pay H. P. Gould, May, 1837, H. Reed, cash, D. Smith, pres., both names in same hand writing.
2's, figure 2 in the centre; female and eagle on the left, three females on the right—impression dark & poorly done.
3's, let. A. Oct. 6, 1837, pay J. Kellogg, P. M. Corbin, cash., Ira Smith, 2d pres. Others, dated 13th Aug. 1837.
10's, let. P & let. B, vig. a steamboat, left end a train of railroad cars; Ira Smith, pres, P. M. Corbin, cash; engraving good—filling up and signing in the same writing.
20's, vig. an agricultural picture, purporting to be engraved by the Eastern Bank Note Engraving Co.

Farmers' & Mech. Bank, Burlington, ... do
[John Peck, Pres., C. F. Warner, Cash.]
☞ Beware of drafts of Mechanics' Exchange Co., New-York, on above Bank, they are FRAUDS.
3's, let. L, pay to Chas. Adams, Aug. 1, 1837.
3's, let. E. Sept. 9, 1837, pay to D. Nash, F. Hockley, cash., and John Peck, pres.
5's, let. E. pay D. Cole, Burlington, Dec. 12, 1837, C. F. Warner, cash., Jno. Peck pres. Others, J. Weekly. cash.
3's, let. L. pay H. Brown, Dec. 4, 1837, C. F. Warner, cash, John Peck, pres, purports to be engraved by A.B. & C. Durand, Wright & Co. Appearance bad.
3's, let. D. May 4, 1837. Chs. Henshaw, pres. H. Broadhead, cash. Others, F. Hockley, cash, John Peck, pres.
5's, altered; vig. a female caressing an eagle.
5's, let. A. May 12, 1830, pay Samuel Blair, C. F. Warner, cash., John Peck, pres.—looks bad, especially the vignettes.
10's, altered, vig. a female, sheaf of wheat, cattle, &c.
50's, altered, vig. figure of Hope. On right end a stag, on left, a female figure, with one foot on a globe.
100's, altered—Lafayette & Washington on the ends.

Green Mountain Bank, ... fraud
Jefferson Banking Co., ... fraud

Orange County Bank, Chelsea, ... ¼
[L. Bacon, Pres., E. C. Redington, Cash.]
☞ For counterfeits see "Bank of Orange County."

Phenix Bank, Philipsborough, ... fraud

Stark Bank, Bennington, ...
[Wm. S. Southworth, Pres., G. W. Harman, Cash.]

Vermont State Bank, [and Branches,] .... fraud

Woodstock Bank, ... ¼
[O. P. Chandler, Pres., E. Johnson, Cash.]

MASSACHUSETTS.

Adams Bank, Adams, (North village,) .... ¼
[Duty S. Tyler, Pres., W. E. Brayton, Cash.]
2's, let. B. has rail cars, &c. General appearance bad.
5's, vig. a female, sheaf of wheat, cow, &c.; looks bad.
10's, vig. an Indian viewing rail cars, under headway

Agawam Bank, Springfield, ... do
[Chester W. Chapin, Pres., F. S. Bailey, Cash.]

Agricultural Bank, Pittsfield, ... do
[Nathan Willis, Pres., E. H. Colt, Cash.]
1's, E. A. Colt, Cr., G. Ford, Pr., these names are not on true bills; vignette, agricultural scene.
2's, vignette a female, sheaf of grain & cattle.
2's, E. W. Beebe cash., J. Davis pres't; these persons never were officers of this bank.
3's, let. A; vig. female and agricultural implements, steamboat and ship in the back ground.
5's, vig. female, vessel, &c—on left end a female with rake.
3's, let. A. pay to H. Burr, dated Jan. 1, 1819.
5's, altered from a broken bank of Belchertown, Mass.

American Bank, Boston, ... Closed
Amherst Bank, ... Charter surrendered

Andover Bank, Andover, ... ¼
[Samuel Farrar, Pres., Francis Cogswell, Cash.]
5's, altered from a broken concern.
10's, altered, engraved by the New Eng. Bank Note Co. The true notes have the check plate on the back.

Appleton Bank, Lowell, ... do
[John A. Knowles, Pres., John A. Buttrick, Cash.]

Asiatic Bank, Salem, ... do
[N. W. Neil, Pres., W. H. Foster, Cash.]

Atlantic Bank, Boston, ... do
[Pliny Cutler, Pres., Benjamin Dodd, Cash.]
1's, let. E, old plate, blurred; pale appearance.
2's, altered from Lafayette Bank of Boston.
5's, altered, Joshua Child, Cash., A. G. Smith, Pres.

Atlas Bank, Boston, ... do
[Samuel C. Gray, Pres., Joseph White, Cash.]
1's, various dates, Gray, pres. Otis, cash.

2's, Perkins' stereotype check plate—irregular and blurred appearance.
3's, counterfeit, let. A., C. Otis, Cash., R. Gray, pres. Jan. 1, 1842. Stereotype plate.
5's, altered, let. C. pay H. Clay—"ATLAS" is def ctive.

Attleborough Bank, Attleborough, ... ¼
[S. Carpenter, Pres., E. Fuller, Cash.]
5's, let. C; vig. a steam car, the goddess of Liberty on the right. Pale appearance
5's, let. in German text; vig. cattle; two "5" on the left end, no figure or V on the right, paper whitish.
10's, vig. female, sitting; two "X" on the left, "ten" on the right. Letter B, in German text.

Bank of Brighton, ... do
[E. Sparhawk, Pres., L. Baldwin, Cash.]
10's, let. C, vig. two ships, right end a steamboat, female on the left. Pay C. Strong, May 4th, 1840.
10's, let. A. pay to C. Strong.

Bank of Gen'l Interest, Salem, ... Closed

Barnstable Bank, Yarmouth, ... ¼
[Isaiah Crowell, Pres., Amos Otis, Cash.]
5's, an alteration; vig. three females.

Bay State Bank, Lawrence, ... do
[C. S. Storrow, Pres., Nathl. White, Cash.]

Bedford Commercial Bk., N. Bedford, ... do
[George Howland, Pres., T. B. White, Cash.]
2's, different letters, and variously filled up.
5's, different letters and dates, and variously filled up.
10's, let. A. n. pay E. Perry, 1st Sept. 1820.
10's, dated Sept. 1824. Others, May 13, 1820.

Berkshire Bank, Pittsfield, ... Closed

Beverly Bank, Beverly, ... ¼
[P. Lovett, Pres., R. G. Bennett, Cash.]
5's, altered; let. A, John Philips, cash. A. Quimby. pres.

Blackstone Bank, Uxbridge, ... do
[Paul Whitin, Pres., E. W. Hayward, Cash.]
5's and 10's, altered from ones; the P in the name of "N.P Denny" does not come down to the line.
50's, altered from 3's—well executed.

Boston Bank, Boston, ... do
[Robert Hooper, Jr. Pres., James C. Wild, Cash.]
2's & 5's, stereotype plate—no genuine of this plate out. The new plate has not been counterfeited yet.
100s, altered from ones.

Boylston Bank, Boston, ... do
[Wm. Parker, Pres., D. McB. Thaxter, Cash.]

Bristol County Bank, Taunton, ... do
[Wm. A. Crocker, Pres., W. Muenscher, Cash.]
5's, altered from a broken Maine bank, well done.
5's, 10's & 20's, altered from genuine ones.

Bunker Hill Bank, Charlestown, ... do
[David Devens, Pres., Thomas Marshall, Cash.]
10's, altered from ones—well done.

Cabot Bank, Cabotville, ... do
[John Chase, Pres., Gilbert Walker, Cash.]
5's, vig. a female, sheaf of grain, &c.—FIVE on the right; a cow on the left. Very unlike the genuine
10's, let. B, vig. a child on a horse, a blacksmith, & a man resting on a wheel holding the horse—female on the left, TEN on the right. The bill has a pale appearance.

Cambridge Bank, Cambridgeport, ... do
[Thomas Whittemore, Pres., Martin Lane, Cash.]

Central Bank, Worcester, ... do
[Thos. Kinnicut, Pres., W. Dickinson, Cash.]
2's, let. A. vig. a female holding a pair of scales—paper whitish. Cashier and president in same hand.

Charles River Bank, Cambridge, ... do
[Chas. C. Little, Pres., J. B. Dana, Cash.]
1's, 2's, 3's, 5's, and 10's, altered from the plate of some broken bank; counterfeit signatures.
2's, let. A; J.P. Dana, cash., Levi Farewell, pres., various dates, fine lettering on the face of note is irregular.
10's, altered from ones.
20's, an alteration—description not known.
50's, altered from 3's.

Charlestown Bank, (redeemed at Suffolk Bank). Closed
Chelsea Bank, ... Closed

Chickopee Bank, Springfield, ... ¼
[Samuel Raynolds, Pres., B F. Warner, Cash.]
3's, vig. a spread eagle—paper feels oily; likely to deceive.
5's, vig. eagle & U.S. coat of arms—female & rail car son the ends
5's, altered from 1's, various dates.

Citizens' Bank, Nantucket, ... Closed
[W. C. Starbuck, Cash.]
1's, 2's, 3's & 5's altered from Citizens' Bk, Augusta, Me.

Citizens' Bank, Worcester, ... ¼
[P. T. Merrick, Pres., G. A. Trumbull, Cash.]
2's and 3's, altered from Citizens' Bank, Augusta, Me. The words Worcester and Massachusetts ditto.

City Bank of Boston, Boston, ... do
[C. W. Cartwright, Pres., J. Williams, Cash.]
10's, let. A, altered from the Roxbury Bank, John Phillips, cash., A. Quimby, prest.

Cohannet Bank, Taunton, ... Closed

MASSACHUSETTS.

Columbian Bank, Boston,............... ½
[John G. Torrey, Pres., Wm. Coffin, Cash.]
2's, altered, signed Joshua Child, cash, Smith, pres.
5's; lett. L. dated Nov. 1st, 1838, pay L. Cushing.
5's, imitation of Perkins' old stereotype plate; "FIVE DOLLARS" in fine print, all over the face of the note, is very crooked and irregular.

Commercial Bank, Salem, ... do
[Wm. Sutton, Pres., E. H. Payson, Cash.]
☞ Beware of bills of all denominations, altered from broken Commercial bank, Millington, Md.
2's, vig. a female, sitting ; Washington on the right end, paper light. Letter A.
2s, 3s, 5s & 10s, altered from a Michigan bank.

Commercial Bank, Boston,...........Charter annulled
Commonwealth Bank, Boston,................Closed
Concord Bank, Concord,........................ ½
[Daniel Shuttuck, Pres., J. M. Cheyney, Cash.]
2's, altered from the bank of the same name in Michigan, by substituting "Mass." for "Mich."
5's, 10's, and smaller denominations, altered from the Sandstone Bank, Jackson Co., Mich.

Danvers Bank, Danvers,....................... do
[E. Shillaber, Pres., G. A. Osborne, Cash.]
50's, altered ; vig. a female feeding an eagle from an urn.

Dedham Bank, Dedham,...................... do
[J. Stimson, Pres., L. H. Kingsbury, Cash.]
5's, let. A. vig. female with a scroll, cars in the distance. The sides have a steamboat and eagle. Paper dark—Tappan Carpenter & Co. N.Y. eng.
10's, description not known.

Dorchester & Milton Bk., Dorchester,..... do
[J. L. Hammond, Cash.]
2's, let. A, Sept. 1, 1832, pay J. Mears.
2's, Aug. 1, 1830, payable to R. Swift.

Duxbury Bank, Duxbury,..............(Closing,) do
☞ Beware of notes altered from the Roxbury Bank.

Eagle Bank of Boston, Boston,............. do
[Titus Welles, Pres., Waldo Flint, Cash.]
2's, let. A. March 16, 1836, pay P. Hambleton. Plate, Perkins stereotype, paper light coloured & rather coarse, impression blurred and irregular, signatures good.
3's, let. A. pay J. P. Blanchard, June 18, 1832.
5s, various letters & dates—payable to different persons.
5s, 10s, & 50s, altered from ones and twos.
10's, altered from ones.
10's, let. I. Engraving irregular, signature of president well done, though rather large.
50's, altered from 1's ; the genuine has 50 on two corners, and L on other two. Altered, 50 on all.
50's, altered from 10's. Clumsily done.

East Bridgewater Bk., E. Bridgewater,...... do
[J. M. Goodwin, Cash.]

Essex Bank, N. Andover,..................... do
[W. Stevens, Cash.]

Essex Bank, Salem,...........................Closed

Exchange Bank, Boston,...................... ½
[G. W. Thayer, Pres., Joseph Marsh, Cash.]

Exchange Bank, Salem,..................... do
[Gideon Tucker, Pres., J. Chadwick, Cash.]
3's, let. B, April 1, 1841, vig. rail car & engine ; Rawdon, Wright & Hatch, N.Y engr.; paper whitish, appears bad.
5's, vig. child sleeping, reaper, dog & grain. Alteration.
20's, let. A. stereotype, signatures engraved.

Fair Haven Bank, Fair Haven,............... ½
[E. Sawin, Pres., Reuben Nye, Cash.]
1's, 2's, 3's, 5's & 10's, purporting to be on this bank, altered from the notes of some broken bank—"FAIR HAVEN BANK" defective.
5's, 10's & 20's, altered from genuine ones.
10's, altered from ones—well done.

Falmouth Bank, Falmouth,.................... ½
[John Jenkins, Pres., S. P. Bourne, Cash.]

Fall River Bank, Fall River,................. do
[D. Anthony, Pres., H. H. Fish, Cash.]

Farmers Bank, Boston,...............Worthless

Farmers & Mech Bank, Adams,..........Closed

Far. & Mech. Bank, Belchertown,........Closed

Fitchburg Bank, Fitchburg,..................
[Francis Perkins, Pres., E. Torrey, Cash.]
10's, let. A. vig. eagle with arrows ; Washington on the left, Indian & female on the right—"10" on each corner.
20's, pay Jno. Boynton, May 1, 1837, F. Perkins, pres.
50's, altered from smaller denominations.

Franklin Bank, Boston,....................Closed

Framingham Bank, Framingham,............ ½
[O. Dean, Pres., Rufus Brewer, Cash.]
10s, altered ; vig. a ship, wheels, &c. cars in the distance.
10s, altered from a Michigan bank ; the genuine are from the patent stereotype plate.

Freeman's Bank, Boston,...................... ½
[Solomon Piper, Pres., Jeremy Drake, Cash.]
50s, description not known.

Fulton Bank, Boston,...................Closed

Globe Bank of Boston, Boston,............. ½
[L Sargent, Pres., Charles Sprague, Cash.]
☞ Beware of small bills of Globe Bank of Bangor, Maine, altered. Parsons and Howard are the officers.
5's, altered from notes of Farmers' Bank, Belchertown. Charles Sprague, cash., J. C. Pray, pres.

Gloucester Bank, Gloucester,................ do
[Isaac Somes, Pres., J. J. Babson, Cash.]
2's, in RED INK—Red bills are not now in use by the bank.
3's, let. B. altered from 1's, Nov. 3, 1829, figure 3 in corner is much more clumsy than genuine. Done in RED INK.
5s, let. K ; the officers names are counterfeited.

Grand Bank, Marblehead,.................... do
[J. Chamberlain, Pres., J. P. Turner, Cash.]
5's, let. M, Jan 4th, 1832, pay J. Newhall.
50's, altered from small bills, vig. a steamboat.

Granite Bank, Boston,....................... do
[George Denny, Pres., Archibald Foster, Cash.]
5s, J.J. Fenton, cash.—no genuine are signed by Fenton.
5's, altered from a broken bank, Geo. Daney, pres.

Greenfield Bank, Greenfield,................. do
[Henry W. Clapp, Pres., Franklin Ripley, Cash.]
10's, lett. A. dated Dec. 7, 1835, pay T. Allen.
10's, lett. A. a. dated Jan. 4, 1838.
10's, let. A. vig. a woman churning, Dec. 8, 1835.

Grey Lock Bank, ...Closed

Hamilton Bank, Boston,..................... ½
[Danl. Denny, Pres., Otis Turner, Jr., Cash.]
1's, 2's, 3's, 5's and 10's, altered from the Lafayette Bank, which has failed.

Hampden Bank, Westfield,................... do
[A. Post, Pres., R. Weller, Cash.]
5s, spurious, vig. a beehive, &c.

Hampshire Manufact'rs' Bk., Ware,........ do
[Joseph Bowman, Pres., William Hyde, Cash.]

Hancock Bank, Boston,..............Charter expired

Haverhill Bank, Haverhill,................... ½
[Hazen Morse, Pres., James Gale, Cash.]
1's, alteration, vig. coat of arms of N. Y.—rail cars and ship in the distance.
2s, altered—"Haverhill Bank" & "Haverhill," defectiv Counterfeit signatures. Altered from some broken bank.
2's, vig. steamboat, &c.; Lafayette, cow & calf to the right.
3's, vig. a group of females, one with a pail on her head ; a vessel in the distance.
3s, vig. vessels & steamboats—locomotive at the bottom.
5s, altered ; vig. Neptune and Venus in a sea-chariot, a steam boat between the signatures.
5's & 10's, altered from 1's and 2's.
20s, altered, vig. blacksmith and forge—rail cars on the left—paper light.

Hingham Bank, Hingham,.................... do
[N. Richards, Pres., John O. Lovett, Cash.]
10's, altered from 1's ; TEN is in the centre of the genuine bill—in the fraud, its on the sides.

Housatonic Bank, Stockbridge,............... do
[Wm. P. Walker, Pres., J. D. Adams, Cash]
☞ This Bank never issued any 20's.

Kilby Bank, Boston,......................Closed
Lafayette Bank, Boston,..................Closed

Lancaster Bank, Lancaster,................. ½
[Jacob Fisher, Pres., C. T. Symmes, Cash.]
10's, an alteration—lion and unicorn between the officers names ; signing bad.

Lee Bank, Lee,............................. do
[Leonard Church, Pres., Thomas Green, Cash.]

Leicester Bank, Leicester,.................. do
[C. Hatch, Pres., H. G. Henshaw, Cash.]
1's, pay Lyman Waite; paper thin and signing poor. O in "ONE," on left end, smaller than the other letters.
2's, dated June 12, 1837, H. G. Henshaw, Cash.
5's, let. K. date & number in pale ink, pay C. Nelson, N.P. Denny, pres. H.G. Henshaw, cash., Jan. 12, 1838.
10's, let. I. various dates, the letter "I" in both 'president' and 'directors,' is not dotted.
10's, let. I, Aug. 10, 1833, pay M. Prime—good imitation.

Lowell Bank, Lowell,....................... do
[Nath. Wright, Pres., David Hyde, Cash.]
5's, an alteration. H. N. Baldwin, Cash.

Lynn Mechanics' Bank, Lynn,.............. do
[J. Breed, Pres., James Oliver, Cash.]

Machinists' Bank, Taunton,................ do
[Wm. Mason, Pres., E R. Anthony, Cash.]

Mahaiwe Bank, Great Barrington,........... do
[Wilbur Curtis, Pres., Henry Hooker, Cash.]

Manufacturers' Bank, Georgetown,......... do
[B. Little, Pres., G. Foot, Cash.]
1's, 2's, 3's, & 5's, alterations, "Manufacturers' Bank" and "Massachusetts" defective.
5's, altered ; vignette, three females.
10's, altered ; vig. U. S. coat of arms ; Indian and a female on right end, and Washington on the left.

Manuf. & Mechan. Bk. Nantucket,....(broke) —

MASSACHUSETTS

Marblehead Bank, Marblehead............ ½
(John Hooper, Pres., S. S. Trefry, Cash.)
2s, Perkins' old stereotype check plate—appears blurred.
Filling up and signatures are bad.
3s, old plate, check letter A. Filling up very bad.
5s, well done. General appearance good.

Market Bank, Boston,...................... do
(J. Stickney, Pres., Jona. Brown, Jr., Cash.)
☞ Spurious bills (supposed to be) of various denominations, altered from the Lafayette Bank.

Marine Bank, New-Bedford,................ do
(Joseph Grinnell, Pres., John P. Barker, Cash.)
3s, vig. vessel under sail—whale scene at the bottom.
10's, altered from a broken Bank.
10s, vig. stream of water ; a vessel under sail on the left

Massachusetts Bank, Boston,............... do
(J. J. Dixwell, Pres., James Dodd, Cash.)
5's, lett. C. pay J. Power, dated Dec. 4th, 1827.
10's, altered from ones—vig. au Indian, sitting.
50s, altered from ones.
100's, altered from 2's, vig. two ships, steamboat & sloop—"one" at top & bottom of bill is spelt OEN

Massasoit Bank, Fall River,............... do

Mechanics' Bank, Newburyport,............ do
J. Andrews, Jr., Cash.)
1's, Perkins' old plate. filling up and signing bad.
2s, stereotype plate; TWO DOLLARS in small type blurred
3's: description hereafter.

Mechanics' Bank, New-Bedford,............ do
(Wm. R. Rodman, Pres., J. Congdon, Cash.)
5's, altered from some other bank of the same name, by substituting the words New-Bedford.

Mechanics' Bank, South Boston,............ do
(David Nickerson, Pres., Alva Simonds, Cash.)
10s, vig. small sail boat & steamboat; Washington on horse back in a circle on the upper right corner—engraving poor.

Mendon Bank,........................ Closed

Mercantile Bank, Salem,.................. ½
(D. Putnam, Pres., S. Webb, Cash.)

Merchants' Bank, Boston,................. do
(Franklin Haven, Pres., John J. May, Cash.)
3s, vig. a lady in a kneeling posture—a man ploughing on the right end, Vulcan on the left.
3's, Cupids on the right, and a man sitting down holding a scroll on the left. General appearance good.
5's, altered from I's Must inspect the back closely.
5's, let. C. pay J. Smith vig. ship undersail ; medallion head of Washington on the right end—the words MASSACHUSETTS SAFETY FUND" on top of the bill.
50's, altered—FIFTY and 50 pasted on. Well done.

Merchants' Bank, New-Bedford,............. ½
(J. A. Parker, Pres., J. B. Congdon, Cash.)
3's, vig. a man with a pencil and scroll ; large 3 on the left, and 3 in the centre.
5's, let. C. pay S. Brown, Aug. 4, 1840 ; vig. two ships, crossing eachother. Cash.'s name in black pres. in blue.
5's, 10's & 20's, altered from genuine ones.
10's, Jan. 4, 1840, pay A. Wood—filling up and signatures blue ink ; vig. a ship undersail, and a brig crossing her wake—between the prest. & cash's names is a brig.

Merchants' Bank, Salem,................... do
(J. W. Treadwell, Pres., F. H. Silsbee, Cash.)
5's, let. C. very large letter, placed between cashier and president's names, on the bottom of the bill, pay to C. Bliss, dated Jan. 9, 1839.

Merchants' Bank, Newburyport,............. do
(Henry Johnson, Pres., Samuel Mullikin, Cash.)
2's, the fine lettering is blurred & irregular.
3's, centre vig. a figure of Solon—on the right end a ship, left end a country girl.
3's, let. A. vig. a painter holding a brush, state house in distance—purports to be engraved by "Draper, Underwood & Co., N.Y."—no such a house in this city.
5's, vig. shipping, &c. Durand & Co. engravers.

Merrimac Bank, Haverhill,................. do
(Rufus Langley, Pres., E. A. Porter, Cash.)
3s, vig. stores, wharfs, loaded wagons, &c. Well done.
5s and 10s, altered from a broken Western concern ; the names of the bank seem as if they had been done with a pen.
10's, an alteration; Drake, cash., Goodrich, prest.
100s, altered from threes.

Middlesex Bank, Cambridge,............... Closing

Middling Interest Bank, Boston,.......... Closed

Millbury Bank, Millbury,................. ½
(S. Farnsworth, Pres., J. Prentiss, Cash.)
3s, vig. steamboat, ships, &c.; rail cars in the left corner.

Nahant Bank, Lynn,...................... Closed

Neponset Bank, Canton,.................. ½
(James Dunbar, Pres., F. W. Deane, Cash.)

Newburyport Bank,....................... Closed

New-England Bank, Boston,................ ½
(Thomas Lamb, Pres., E. P. Clark, Cash.)
1's, let. E on right hand end, lett. O on both ends.
2's, let. A, paper thin; engraving rather blured, and the fine print which covers the face of the note is irregular. Various dates.
3's, let. A., No. 145, March 1, 1841, pay J. Swan, E. P. Clarke, Cash, Ph. Meritt, Pres. "Check letter" round the letter A. Stereotype plate, paper whitish.

Nuumkeag Bank, Salem,..................... ½
(D. Pingree, Pres., J. G. Sprague, Cash.)
5s, 10s, 20 & 50s, altered front 3s, vig. view of banking house ; vessels on the left. Terry, Pelton & Co., engrav.

North Bank of Boston, Boston,............ do
(James Harris, Pres., J. J. Loring, Cash.)
3's, let. L. Sep. 20,1831, pay Wm. M Cray—G. Steele, cash, J. Binney, pres ; "II" in Massachusetts has no crossstroke.
50's, 100's & 500's, altered from 1s, vig. State House, ship on the left—"one," at top & bottom is spelt "OEN."

Norfolk Bank, Roxbury................... Closed

Northampton Bank, Northampton........... ½
(E. Williams, Pres., J. D. Whitney, Cash.)
☞ This bank has withdrawn all its notes of the counterfeited plate, and is issuing new bills dated April 1, 1845, and subsequently. All notes out of a previous date had better be rejected.
1's, 3's, & 5's, altered ; hold them to the light.
5's, let. F. altered from the plate of a broken bank—"Northampton" before the date is of slanting letter, in the genuine the letter is perpendicular.

Ocean Bank, Newburyport,................. do
(Ebenezer Hale, Pres., Jacob Stone, Cash.)
5's, let. C. vig. and die work light and coarse.
10's, altered ; vig two females, a boy with cap, & negro boy, Franklin & rail car on left ; paper quite white. The body of the genuine is covered with fine printing, better be rejected.

Old Colony Bank, Plymouth,............... do
(J. B. Thomas, Pres., S. Sampson, Cash.)
50's, altered from ones.

Oriental Bank, Boston,................... Closed

Oxford Bank, Oxford,..................... ½
(A. De Witt, Pres., A. G. Underwood, Cash.)
5's altered from Oxford Bank, Fryeburg, Me.

Pacific Bank, Nantucket,................. do
(F. W. Mitchell, Pres., Wm. Mitchell, Cash.)
2s, altered, vig. f-male in a sitting posture ; anchor, &c. between the names of the officers.
5s, an alteration—vig. shipping, &c.
10s. altered, vig. rail cars, and four persons sitting down.

Pawtucket Bank, Pawtucket,............... do
(J. O. Starkweather, Pres., A. A. Tillinghast, Cash.)
5's, an alteration, vig. a female nursing a child.
10's, altered, vig. declaration of independence.
50's, vig. lady, eagle and vase : "Pawtucket Bank" looks suspicious.—It is an alteration.

People's Bank, Roxbury,.................. do
(Samuel Guild, Pres., B. Stone, Cash.)
1's, engraved on the stereotype plate. Beware of bills altered from Roxbury Bank, to " PEOPLE'S BANK OF ROXBURY"—John Phillips cash., A. Quimby, pres.

Phœnix Bank, Charlestown,................ Closed
Phenix Bank, Nantucket,.................. Closed

Plymouth Bank, Plymouth,................. ½
(Nathaniel M. Davis, Pres., J. N. Stoddard, Cash.)
1's, let. E., May 2, 1841, blurred appearance.
1's, let. E., Mar. 20, 1842, E. and D. on each end.
2's, let. A., June 1, 1841 and 2, pay to W. C. Clark. Others, Nov. 6, 1842, pay J. Peck.
3's, counterfeit, let. A., various dates. The words "Three Dollars," in fine print, defective

Powow River Bank, Salisbury,............. do
(Seth Clark, Pres., N. White, Cash.)

Quinnebaug Bank, Worcester,.............. do
(Wm. Jennison, Pres., C. A. Hamilton, Cash.)

Quincy Stone Bank, Quincy,............... do
(Lemuel Brackett, Pres., J. Bartlett, Cash.)
1's, altered—vig. female holding a rake & sickle, ship in the distance.
5's, altered—vig. three females, head of Franklin on the left end and Lafayette on the right.
10's, vig. spread eagle—Washington on the left.
20's, altered from twos, well executed.
50's, altered from small bills. Well done.

Rail Road Bank, Lowell,.................. do
(B. F. French, Pres., S. W. Stickney, Cash.)
5's, let. C, various dates ; T. W. Stickney, cash., P. W. Warren, pres. Payable to C. Aiken.
5's, vig. railroad & boat ; lady on the right, Indian on the left—whitish paper.
10's, altered from 5's. Well done
20's, let. A. vig. rail cars ; a woman on the left end.

Randolph Bank, Randolph,................. do
(R. Turner, Pres., Seth Turner, Cash.)
1s, vig. a female sitting, with sheaf of grain, sickle, &c. has the words "real esale pledged," in upper right corner, & " one " five times on the lower margin—filling up poor. Underwood, Bald, Spencer & Hufty, eng'vrs. An alteration.
3s, alteration. vig. Indian sitting down, and a deer between the officers names.
5s, alt red, vig. a female holding an infant, with reapers in the distance—a locomotive and rail cars under the word " Massachusetts,"—Danforth, Underwood & Co. engravers.
10s, vig. declaration of independence—a blacksmith on the right end, and a man with a flag, and vessels on the left.

Roxbury Bank,........................... Closed

Salem Bank, Salem,....................... do
(Geo. Peabody, Pres., C. M. Endicott, Cash.)

Shawmut Bank, Boston,.................... do
(Benj. T. Reed, Pres., Thomas Drown, Cash.)
5's, altered from 1's—hold them to the light.

Shoe & Leather Dealers' Bank, Boston,.... do
(Enoch Baldwin, Pres., Geo. W. Thayer, Cash.)
50's & 100s, altered from ones.

South Bridge Bank, South Bridge,............ ¼
 [S. A. Hitchcock, Pres., S. M. Lane, Cash.]

South Bank of Boston,............(Closing) do
 [B. C. Clark, Pres., J. J. Loring, Cash.]
 10's and **50's,** altered from **1's.**

Springfield Bank, Springfield,................ do
 [John Howard, Pres. Lewis Warriner, Cash.]

State Bank, Boston,........................... do
 [Sam. Frothingham, Pres., Jonathan Call, Cash.]
 2's, the genuine bill has "MASSACHUSETTS" over the centre, the spurious has it at the end, not over the centre.
 3's, dated Sept. 4th, 1826, payable to J. Cross.
 5's, vig. a group of faces encircling the 5—lithograph.
 5's, engraving very coarse, and signing bad.
 10's, altered from ones of the same bank.
 10's, lett. A. pay C. Warner, June 15, 1840.
 10's, Jan. 1st, 1834, J. P. Sutton, cash. President's name written in pale ink, and not legible. Easily told by a red oval in the centre.
 10's, lett. I. pay to J. Cull, dated Dec. 2, 1835.
 10's, lett. I. dated April 12th, 1837. Perkins' steel plate, engraving irregular.
 10's, E. A. Bourne, pres., Geo. Homer, cash.—various dates, and payable to different persons.
 10's, lett. C. well executed, pay J. Coolridge, June 30, 1823. They have a red oval in the centre.

Suffolk Bank of Boston, Boston,............ do
 [Hy. B. Stone, Pres., Isaac C. Brewer, Cash.]
 2's, lett. A, check plate, blur under ' bank."
 3's, lett. A, Oct. 2, 1841, pay S. Jones—the fine print is very irregular. Others with different dates.
 5's, lett. L., facsimile of genuine; engraving light—name of the bank looks bad.
 5's, lett. L; Curtis Pattee, Jas. Lansing, officers.
 5's, lett. M., July 22, 1835, No. 590.
 5's, lett. R., Jas. Adams, cash, R. W. Benton, pres.
 5's, filling up in pale ink, the fine print irregular.
 5's, altered from Belchertown Bank, cashier's name Lyman, is altered to WYMAN, and the initials blotted.
 10's, lett. L. paper a dull yellow, impression poor. J. C. Brewer, cash., Henry B. Stone, pres.
 10's, pay to H. B. Stone, dated April 9, 1831.
 10's, purporting to be of Perkins' stereotype steel plate—fall an inch shorter than the genuine notes—the engraving is faint and indistinct.
 10's, lett. L—the cashier's name is written below the line—pay E. Cook.
 100's, lett. A. vig. locomotive, &c. Danforth, Spencer & Hasty, never engraved for this Bank.

Sutton Bank, Wilkinsonville,..............Closed

Taunton Bank, Taunton,............... ¼
 [Ellis Hall, Pres., C. J. H. Bassett, Cash.]
 5's, lett. A. vig. a lady, sheaf of wheat, &c., an ox and two V's on the right, & FIVE on left end.
 10's, vig. a man shoeing a horse, a boy at his side.
 20's, lett. A. vig. locomotive, shrub to the right; a female on the left; eagle, nest and young at the bottom. C. J. H. Bassett, cash., Ellis Hale, pres, in same still hand.
 50's, lett. A. vign'e a female and agricultural implements. Pale and dark appearance.
 50's, altered, "the Taunton Bank" defective—hold to the light. Vignette, a female, eagle, &c.

Traders' Bank, Boston,.................. do
 [Isaac Parker, Pres., Jeremiah Gore, Cash.]
 5's, altered from Comm. Bank, Millington, Md. The word "Boston" is very defective. All bills signed W. Adams, Cash., and H. Mead, Pres., are alterations from the above bank.

Tremont Bank, Boston,..................... do
 [Andrew T. Hall, Pres., A. T. Frothingham, Cash.]
 10's, altered from the old Franklin Bank.

Union Bk. of Weymouth, Weymouth,...... do
 [Benj. King, Pres., Tbs. B. Hanson, Cash.]

Union Bank, Boston,....................... do
 [Chester Adams, Pres., Chester Adams, Cash.]
 5's, lett. E. pay to N. Emmons, May 13, 1823.
 5's, lett. E. pay to N. Smith, dated Nov. 1, 1823.
 5's, lett. E. dated Jan. 1, 1821, pay to S. Sloan.

Village Bank, Danvers,..................... do
 [Moses Putnam, Pres., W. L. Weston, Cash.]
 10's, altered from ones.

Waltham Bank, Waltham .... do
 [Chas. Bemis, Pres., N. Maynard, Cash.]
 5's & 10's, altered from ones—well done.
 10's, altered, "the Waltham Bank," stamped on.

Warren Bank, Danvers,................... do
 [E. W. Upton, Pres., F. Baker, Cash.]
 5's, vig. steamboat and sail vessels, with Washington and Franklin on the right and also on the left end.
 5's, lett. A, vig. a female, sickle, sheaf of grain, &c., rail cars in distance—FIVE on the right, a cow & two V's on left.

Warren Bank, [now the Shawmut Bank,]

Wareham Bank, Wareham,................ do
 [Peter Mackie, Pres., Thos. R. Mills, Cash.]

Washington Bank, Boston,................ ¼
 [Aaron Baldwin, Pres., D. A. Sigourny, Cash.]
 1's, lett. E, "check letter" round it—"Washington Bank" defective. Others, same letter. (E.)
 2's, lett. A.—the C in "Massachusetts," stands higher than the other letters.
 3's, counterfeit, lett. A.—pay Fny. Perkins' old stereotype plate, Dec. 2, 1841. Others, March 26.
 5's, check let. Limitation of Perkins' old stereo. plate.
 10's an alteration; vig. an eagle, &c.

Winthrop Bank, Roxbury,................. do
 [J. Russell, Cash.]
 2's, lett. D. dated April 21, 1838, payable to Ed. Curtis, James Russell, cash., John J. Clark pres.
 5's, altered from the Roxbury B'nk—the word WINTHROP in place of "Roxbury" before Bank.
 100's, altered, the words, the WINTHROP BANK, appear to have been inserted in the place of "ROXBURY."

Wiscasset Bank,.......................Worthless

Worcester Bank, Worcester,............... ¼
 [S. Salisbury, Pres., Samuel Jennison, Cash.]
 2's, lett. A. Perkins' plate. Appears blurred
 3's, lett. A. pay J. Brooks or bearer. Aug. 3, 1819; paper very light colored. Samuel Jennison, cash.
 5's, lett. A, vig. a blacksmith, pay J. Wilson, Sept. 1, 1826.

Wrentham Bank, Wrentham,.............. do
 [John Tifft, Pres., Calvin Fisher, Jr. Cash.]
 1's, altered from some broken bank.
 2's, an alteration; hold them to the light.

RHODE ISLAND.

American Bank, Providence,............... ¼
 [H. P. Franklin, Pres., S. K. Rathbone, Cash.]
 10's, altered, vig. an eagle and shield ; Washington on the left end, and an Indian on the right.

Arcade Bank, Providence,.................. do
 [Paris Hill, Pres., Jos. Hodges, Cash.]
 1's, an alteration; vig. a dog and sleeping child.
 2's, vig. a giant, sitting; "ARCADE" defective; altered from a broken b'k, counterfeit signatures.
 5's, altered from a broken bank note—vig. a female holding a child—"Arcade Bank" defective.
 10's, an alteration; vig. signing the declaration of independence;" Arcade Bank" defective.

Bank of Bristol,........................... do
 [Mark Anth'y. D'Wolf, Pres., M. Bennett, Cash.]
 10's, altered from 2's; vig apread-eagle, "Bank of Bristol" defective. " Rhode Island" and "Bristol" stamped on.

Bank of North America, Providence,........ do
 [Elisha Harris, Pres., H. E. Hudson, Cash.]
 10's, alt'd from 2's, old plate; Cyrus Butler pres.
 50's, & 100's, altered from 5's, old plate, engraved by Reed & Pelton.

Bank of Kent, Coventry,................... do
 [Peleg Wilbur, Pres., Anthony Tarbox, Cash.]
 3's, lett. A. pay to P. Tillinghast, April 1, 1819.
 3's, lett. C. dated April 1, 1819.

Bank of Rhode Island, Newport,............ do
 [Peleg Clarke, Pres., Wm. A. Clarke, Cash.]
 ☞ ALL notes signed J. Munson and P. King, are spurious, they never were officers of this bank.
 1's, old plate, pay J. Hammond, Jan. 20, 1831.
 2's, lett. B. Jan. 14, 1831, pay Wm. Rotch, S. Fowler, Gardner, Cash., Andely Clark, Pres.
 5's, lett. C. July 20, 1837, pay S. Jones—vig. rail cars—an Indian on each end. No resemblance to the genuine.
 10's, lett. A. dated July 2d, 1839, pay L. Jones,—P. King, Cash., L. Munson, Pres. Unlike the genuine.

Blackstone Canal Bank, Providence,........ do
 [J. C. Brown, Pres. D. W. Vaughn.., Cash.]
 5's & 10's, alt'd from the Stillwater Canal Bank, vignette sawmills, &c. E. P. Butler, cash.
 10's, altered from 1's, calculated to deceive.
 50's, altered from 5's, vig. a female sitting on a rock, filling up in red ink—space between "pay" and "fifty" too small. Well calculated to deceive—no visible defect where the alteration is made.

Bristol Union Bk, [See Fall River Union Bank.]

Burrillville Bank, ...Worthless

Centreville Bank, Warwick,................ ¼
 [John Green, Pres., M. Fifield, Cash.]
 2's, lett. A, vig. a female, with grain, cattle, &c. Paper light, engraving coarse. Reaper on the left end, and female on the right.

Citizens' Union Bank, Scituate,............ do
 [Ashael Harris, Pres., J. A. Harris, Cash.]
 1's, lett. C. pay to bearer, June 4, 1835, D. H. Braman, cash., Josiah (some Joseph) Westcott, pres. Engraving bad, especially the vignette.
 1's, 3's & 5's, lett. B. July. 1836, pay Adam Windsor.

RHODE ISLAND.

City Bank, Providence,........................ ½
  ...., Pres., Henry Earle, Cash.]
  2's, let. A. pay Isaac Case, Nov. 1, 1837, Wm. R. Watson, cash., A. B. Arnold, pres. Appears light & coarse.

Commercial Bank, Bristol,.................... do
  [Jacob Babbitt, jr., Pres.; J. F. Baars, Cash.]
  ☞ Bills of ALL denominations, on this Bank, altered from broken Commercial Bank, Millington, Md.
  2's, lett. C. pay to C. Babbitt, date illegible.
  3's. No State mentioned.
  2's, 3's, 5's & 10's, altered from a broken Mich. bank.
  5's, lett. C. vig. a ship; rail cars at the left, Washington with a horse at the right of the vignette
  5s, altered, with FIVE in red letters, at the bottom.
  5s, vig. a ship under sail—BRISTOL inserted.
  10's, let. D. vig. a ship; a female with a born of plenty on the left, and a wharf scene on the right.

Commercial Bank, Providence,............... ½
  [R. Bullock, Pres., D. Andrews, Cash.]
  ☞ Bills of ALL denominations, on this bank, altered from broken Commercial Bank, Millington Md.
  2's, 3's, 5's & 10's, altered from a broken Mich. bank.
  3s, altered, vig. steamboat, &c.—town in the distance; Washington on left end, female & eagle on right.
  10's, altered from 1's, vig. a steersman—"ONE DOLLAR," in small letters in the margin, is blotted out.

Cranston Bank, Cranston,.................... ½
  [Joseph Harr's, Pres., A. B. Bailey, Cash.]
  3's, pay to C. Baker, Nov. 27, 1828, and some in 1829.
  True bills of that emission, March 20, 1827.
  3's, lett. A. pay B. Harris, dated March 8, 1828.
  3's, pay to B. Harris, dated June 3, 1830.
  5's, altered from a broken bank, vig. 3 females.
  10's, vig. eagle and shield—on the left a small head of Washington, on the right an Indian.

Cumberland Bank, Cumberland,............ ½
  [Davis Cook, Pres., Geo. Cook, Cash.]
  1's, let. C. dated Sept. 15, 1827, Asa Ballad. cash., S Weatherhead, pres.
  2's, lett. C. pay to P. Thomas, Sept. 12, 1825.
  5's, let. A. vig. a female with a sheaf of grain, train of cars in the distance. Engraving bad, paper poor.
  10's, counterfeit, vig. four figures sitting on a globe; cars on the left; "Cumberland," defective.

Eagle Bank of Bristol, Bristol,............... do
  [Jas. Le Baron, Pres., J. E. French, Cash.]
  10's, vig. an eagle holding a shield in his beak, Washington and a cupid on the left end.

Eagle Bank, Providence,...................... do
  [B. D. Weeden, Pres., S.S. Wardwell, Cash.]
  3's, counterfeit, made payable to different persons.
  10's, altered from 1's. The word "twenty," and the figures "20," have a pale appearance.
  20's, altered from 3's—hold them up to the light.

Eagle Bank, Newport,.................Worthless

Exchange Bank, Providence,.................. ½
  [Benj. Aborn, Pres., Hy. G. Gladding, Cash.]
  1's, let. A. pale appearance, engraving on the ends coarse. Vignette, a female.
  3's, lett. A. pay to P. Allen, dated April 3, 1835.
  5's, altered from 1's. Well executed.
  10's, altered from 1's.

Exeter Bank, Exeter,........................... do
  [C.C. Greene, Pres., Thos. Phillips, Cash.]
  3's, lett. B, vig. a ship & female, paper of a yellowish cast.
  5's, lett. C. vign'te cars and locomotive, dock, water, and skiff ½ front; left end an Indian, right end woman with a staff; an Indian in a canoe at the bottom—Thos. Phillips, cash. s. Tillinghast, pres. complexion light, paper thin—Harris & Sealy, engravers.
  10's, has a female and vessel; Iudian & boat at the bottom.

Fall River Union Bank, Tiverton,.......... ½
  [N. B. Borden, Pres., W. Coggeshall, Cash.]
  1's, an alteration; vig. a female holding a rake.
  2's, lett. A. Nov. 10, 1836, pay Jessy Cady; Wm. Coggeshall, cash.
  3's, an alteration; hold them to the light.
  5's & 10's, an alteration; vig. a stream of water with saw mills each side. E. P. Butler, cashier.

Farmers' Exch. Bank, Gloncestor,........Worthless
Farm. & Mech. Bank, Pawtucket,........Worthless

Franklin Bank, Chepachet,.................... ½
  [Job Armstrong, Pres., A. A. Eddy, Cash.]
  1's, lett. B., Oct. 5, 1822, sig'd. one hand writing.
  3's, lett. A. pay to J. Corke, S. Cooke, cash., Jesse Tourtellor, Pres. Blue paper.
  2's, July 9, 1826. Part blue, others white paper.
  2's, let. A. pay C. Day, dated Sept. 27, 1837, signed I. Rhodes, cash., C. Earle, pres.

Franklin Bank, Providence,.............Worthless

Freeman's Bank, Bristol,................... ½
  [Nathl. Bullock, Pres., L. C. Richmond, Cash.]
  5's, 10's & 20's, altered from plate of the Citizens' Bank of Augusta, Me., so well done that good Judges have taken them. Engraved by Terry, Pelton & Co.
  The safe way is to reject all bills engraved by this Co. The bank has issued a new plate by Reed—it is good

Globe Bank, Providence,...................... do
  [Wm. Sprague, Pres., J. L. Noyes, Cash.]
  Beware of bills, altered f'm Globe Bank, Bangor, Me., also Globe Bank, N. Y, S.D. Day, cash, N. Bishop, pres.
  3's, lett. A., vignette, an Indian.
  5's, altered from the Globe Bank, Bangor, Me.

Globe Bank, Smithfield,........................ do
  [Spencer Mowry, Pres., S. Newton, Cash.]

Hamilton Bank, Scituate,.................. fraud

High-Street Bank, Providence,............... ½
  [Robert Knight, Pres., Jas. E. Butts, Cash.]
  100's, altered from smaller bills; vig. 2 blacksmiths at work; the "C" on each side is of a singular shape.

Hope Bank, Warren,........................... do
  [J. Smith, Pres., Thos. C. Williams, Cash.]
  2's, let. B. new plate, Dec. 20, 1821; others, let. B. 1822, and Dec. 10, 1824.

Landholders' Bank, S. Kingston,............ do
  [E. R. Potter, Pres., Ths. R. Wells, Cash.]
  2's, let. A. dated Oct. 4, 1824, pay to C. Bates.
  2's, let. B. Aug. 1, 1823, pay to R. Clark, Elisha R. Potter, pres., Thos. R. Wells, cash.
  2's, let. A. dated South Kingston, Feb. 9, 1836, signed Thos. W. Wells, cash., Thos. S. Taylor, pres.
  5's, let. A. Thos. W. Watts, cash., Thos. G. Taylor, pres. The work is badly done.

Manufacturers' Bank, Providence,......... do
  [Thos. Harkness, Pres., Wm. S. Patten, Cash.]
  3's, lett. A. pay to S. Green, dated Jan. 7, 1825.
  3's, lett. A. pay to H. T. Tiffany, dated Oct. 1, 1827, red ink, and some black. Pardon Sayles, Cash., Samuel Slater, Pres. Others, Aug. 5, 1829.
  5's, let. A. vig. a figure of Justice, a ship under sail; Pardon Sayles, Cash., Sam. Slater, Pres.

Mechanics' Bank, Providence,............... do
  [Amasa Manton, Pres., John A Field, Cash.]
  5's, letts. A. and B. altered from 1's. Josiah Lawton, Cash., January 1, 1828 Feb. 1, 1829, and other dates. Other 5's Sept. 3, 1830, pay to S. B Wood.

Mechanics' & Manuf. Bk., Providence,...... do
  [S. G. Martin, Pres., Albert W. Snow, Cash.]

Merchants' Bank, Newport,.................. do
  [Isaac Gould, Pres., Charles Gyles, Cash.]
  2's, lett. A. spurious, dated May 1, 1824, signed Ben. Howard, Pres, Peter Sampson, Cash.
  3s & 5s, vig. a man, temple, &c.; 3 on left end—steamship between the signatures of Chas. Gyles and W.S. Ruggles
  5's, altered from 1's. The genuine have a view of the State House—the altered have an eagle & paper mill.

Merchants' Bank, Providence,............... ½
  [Wm. Richmond, 2d, Pres. Wm. B. Burdick, Cash.]
  5's, W. Richmond, 2d, Pres., H. E. Hudson, Cash.
  5's, let. A. pay to J. B. Wood, Sept. 3, 1829, James Wheelock, Cash., Wm. Richmond, Pres.
  5's, let. A. pay S. B. Wood, dated Nov. 1, 1830.
  5's, let. C. pay Jno. Green, April 10, 1838. Others, pay o different persons, & of different dates; poorly signed.
  10's, let. A. dated May 29, 1818, J. Wheelock, cash. Wm. Richmond, second, Pres.
  10's, lett. A. pay N. Tangley, May 20, 1819.
  10's, lett. A. pay Luke Green, Nov. 7, 1827.

Mount Hope Bank, Bristol,..............Worthless

Mount Vernon Bank, Foster,.................. ½
  [Sam. Tillinghast, Pres., R. G. Place, Cash.]
  1's, 3's & 5's, altered from a broken bank, by cutting out first name, and inserting the above. Well done.

Narragansett Bank, Wickford,................ do
  [E. D. Davis, Pres., N. N. Spink, Cash.]

National Bank, Providence,................... do
  [o. W. Hallett, Pres., E. Bourn, Cash.]
  2's, lett. A. June 12, 1840, B. Bourn, Cash., E. Wade, Pres. Vignette, two female figures.
  5's, vig. heads of five of the presidents. There are counterfeits with and without RED figures; whitish paper and blurred appearance.
  5's, altered from 1's. Easily detected.
  10's, altered from twos, old plate.

N. England Commercial Bk., Newport,..... ½
  [Geo. Bowen, Pres., Geo T. Weaver, Cash.]
  1's, let. E. pay B. Hazard or bearer, May 1, 1821.
  1's, let. B. pay J. R. Miles, dated Sept. 5, 1826, G. T. Weaver, Cash., Wm. Ennis, Pres.

CONNECTICUT

N. England Pacific Bk., N. Providence,...... ¼
[Jos. Metcalf, Pres., S. Cook, Cash.]

Newport Bank, Newport,....................... do
[Wm. Vernon, Pres., S. Cahoone, Cash.]
1's, lett. A. pay R. Riker, dated July 1, 1837; S. Cahoone, Cash., Wm. Vernon, Pres.
2's, let. C, engrav'd hy Terry, Pelton & Co.—genu. by Fairman, Draper, Underwood & Co. Others, let. B, engraving pale—words "RHODE ISLAND" on the left hand of the good note—the counterfeit has the word two.
5's & **10**'s, altered—vig. a stream of water & mills on each side.—E. P. Butler cash., (not on the genuine.)

North Kingston Bank, Wickford, ... do
[J. Reynolds, Pres., P. T. Hammond, Cash.]
10's, vignette a ship under sail—the words "North Kingston Bank" are crowded close together.

Newport Exchange Bank, Newport,........ do
[N. Hammett, Pres., John Sterne, Cash.]
5's & **10**'s, altered from a broken Maine bank, saw mills for a vignette, E. P. Butler, cash.

North Providence Bank, N. Providence,...... do
[G. L. Spencer, Pres., J. C. Tower, Cash.]
5's, let. B. altered from 1's, E. Bourn, Cash., E. Wade, Pres. July 31, 1840. Others, payable to T. Brown; R. Holden, Cash., Benj. Aborn, Pres.

Pawtuxet Bank, Providence, ... do
[Christo. Rhodes, Pres., T. R. Green, Cash.]
1's, let. B. vig. a bee hive & female, coarse and faint; pay J. Cole, June 7, 1839. Paper oily.
1's, lett. A. pay to Wm. Rhodes, Jan. 1, 1818. Others, 1819; others, pay S. Smith, March 1, 1819.
1's, has "of" instead of "on," before "demand."
1's, lett. A. pay to D. C. Wilbur, Oct. 9, 1837.

Pascoag Bank, Pascoag Village,......(Closing,)

People's Bank of North Providence,...... ¼
[C. F. Manchester, Pres., J. S. Tourtellot, Cash.]

Phoenix Bank, Westerly....................... do
[R. Babcock, Pres., Ethan Foster, Cash.]
1's, **2**'s, **3**'s & **5**'s, altered from the broken Citizens' B'k, A'a., Me. Foster, Cash., Thomas, Pres.
2's, lett. A. July 20, 1837, pay A. Banks, Chas. Peny, ch. Nathan F. Dixon, pres. Others, pay Jas. Mott, July 4, 1837, E. Foster, Jr. Cash., R. Babcock, pres, Rawdon, Wright, Hatch & Co. engravers.
2's, dated Aug. 26, 1837. The letter N in the word ON, preceding demand, is reversed thus, ou.
5's, vig. 3 females. Terry. Pelton & Co., engravers.
20's, altered from 1's. "Twenty Dollars," in plain capitals; the true bill has German text.

Phenix Bank, Providence,.................... do
[S. B. Wheaton. Pres., Benj. White, Cash.]
1's, **2**'s, **3**'s, **5**'s & **10**'s, altered. The word "Citizen" extracted and "Phoenix" inserted.
50's, altered from a 1—vig. ship under full sail.

Providence Bank, Providence,................ do
[Moses B. Ives. Pres., C. L. Bowler. Cash.]
1's, let. C. pay E. Gray, April 12, 1830, No. 397—vig. a woman, sheaves of wheat and implements of agriculture. Very coarsely done, paper white.
3's, spurious, lett. C. dated July 26, 1839, pay to Isaac Case. Paper white and flimsy.
5's, old plate, No. 596, Feb. 25, 1830. Others, let. B. No. 245; paper redder than genuine. Genuine not numbered over 100, of any denomination.
10's, let. A. old plate, pay O. Hawkins. Oct. 27, 1826.
20's, altered from 2's. To detect which, observe that the letters and figures are cramped.
50's & **100**'s, altered from ones, old plate, calculated to deceive good judges. The vig. of the genuine 1's, 2's, and 3's, is a female figure in a sitting position. The genuine 50's & 100's have two female figures with their faces divided by a shield.

Rhode Isl. Central B., E. Greenwich............ do
[Wm. Reynolds, Pres., Lemuel Burge, Cash.]

Rhode Island Union Bank, Newport........ do
[Charles Devens, Pres, Benj. A. Mason, Cash.]
2's, lett. B. old plate, pay C. Stewart. Jan. 1815.
3's, lett. B. old plate, to whom pay, &c. unk.
5's, vig. a ship in a circle.
10's, let. D. signed Geo. C. Mason, cash., Geo. Enga, pres't.—good engraving. The name "Rhode Island Union Bank" has a dark and suspicious look.

Roger Williams' Bank, Providence,.......... do
[N. R. Knight, Pres., Nathaniel Smith, Cash.]
5's, altered from 1's—well executed. Plate of 1's, central vignette, a female figure with trident.
10's, altered from 1's. Excellent imitation.
20's, altered from 1's, vig. a female holding a trident.

Scituate Bank,......................Worthless

Smithfield Exch. Bank, Smithfield........... ¼
[Owen Battey, Pres., Wm. Winsor, Cash.]
1's, old plate; let. A; engraving very poor.
1s, let. A, Jan. 1, 1845, N. Windsor, cash. instead of N.S. Windsor

Smithfield Lime Rock Bk., Smithfield,...... do
[Geo. Olney, Pres., Geo. L. Barnes. Cash.]
3's, June 12, 1838. Geo. Olney, pres, Geo L. Barnes, cash.

Smithfield Union Bank, Smithfield........... do
[John Osborne, Pres., E. T. Rend, Cash.]

Traders' Bank, Newport,...................... do
[Edwin Wilbur, Pres., B. Mumford, Cash.]
5's, altered from a broken Maine bank, vig. 3 females. "The Traders Bank" and "Newport," defective.
50's, altered from a broken Maine bank, vig. a female and eagle—hold them to the light.

Traders' Bank, Providence,................... do
[Karl Carpenter, Pres., H. A. Webb, Cash.]
5's, an alteration—vig. three females.
10's, vig. two females and an animal on a chest; steamboat, ship &c. on the left end, and a female on the right. TEN DOLLARS, in the centre of the note, is poorly done.
50's, same as on "Tratlers' Bank, Newport."

Union Bank, Providence,...................... do
[Elisha Dyer, Pres., J. B. Hoskins, Cash.]
1's, signature is engraved, Jas. B. Hoskins.
5's, lett. A., pay S. Allen, Aug. 1, 1842, No. 1361.
10's, alt'd from 2's, vig. of genuine 2's and alteredd tens a blacksmith and two females.

Village Bank. Smithfield..................... do
[W. S. Slater, Pres., Wm. H. Seagrave, Cash.]
5's, altered, vig. female, sheaf of wheat, cars in distance. A cow on the left. "The Village Bank," slightly defective.
10's, let. B, vig. blacksmith shoeing a horse & a man holding him. A female on the left & TEN on the right. An "X" on each corner of left end, and on each side of the vignette. The hill is well calculated to deceive.

Wakefield Bank, Wakefield................... do
[Syl. Robinson, Pres. T. P. Wells, Cash.]
10's, altered from a worthless bank, vig. an eagle; on the left end a small portrait of Washington.

Warren Bank, Warren,....................... do
[N. M. Wheaton, Pres., George W. Carr, Cash.]

Warwick Bank, Warwick,..................... do
[Wm. D. Brayton, Pres., J. Westcott, Cash.]

Washington Bank, Westerly,................. do
[Nathan F. Dixon, Pres., Charles Perry, Cash.]
2's, pay J. Q. Adams, 4th March, 1841.
3's, pay O. M. Silliman, Nov. 13, 1829.
5's, dated Oct. 1, 1832, my Thomas N'oyes
5's, lett. B. Dec. 15, 1842, and other ates.
10's, altered; hold them to the light.
10's, old plate—John Coffin, cash.—paper thin.

Weybosset Bank, Providence,................. do
[Wm. Rhodes, Pres., Luke Green, Cash.]
2's, let. A. various dates, pay Geo. Ontley, others, pay E. F. Allen, L. Green, Cash., Wm. Rhodes, Pres. The general appearance pale, and letters irregular.

Woonsocket Falls Bank, Cumberland,...... do
[Dexter Ballou, Pres., Wm. Metcalf, Cash.]

CONNECTICUT.

Bridgeport Bank, Bridgeport,................. ¼
[Silv. Sterling, Pres., Geo. Burroughs, Cash.]
5's, let. B. pay L. Berr—Sylvanus Sterling, pres. Badly done.
10's, **20**'s and **50**'s, altered from 1 s, 2's, 3's or 5's. Hold them to the light.

Bridgeport Manufacturing Co.,..........Worthless
Bridgeport Ex. Assoc., ...Worthless

City Bank, New-Haven........................ ¼
[Ezra C. Read, Pres., S. D. Pardee, Cash.]
5's, spurious, Bacon, Cash., Atwater, Pres. Vignette, two steamboats; railroad on left end.

Commercial Bank of Tolland,.........Worthless

Connecticut Bank, Bridgeport,................. ¼
[Daniel Thatcher, Pres., Charles Foote, Cash.]
5's, altered—vig. Neptune and a lady in a sea-carriage, drawn by sea-horses.
5's, altered from a broken bank — "Connecticut Bank" is defective; vig. a female.
10's, altered; vig. Neptune, with car & sea-horses; left end, sailor holding a flag.
10's, let. A. vignette a female resting on a sheaf of wheat; Chas. Foote, ca'h; Danl. Thatcher, Pres.
20's, let. A; vig. female, sheaf of grain, plough, &c.; Indian between the officers names; engraved by Durand & Co. N. Y.

CONNECTICUT.

Connecticut Bank, Southport, ... ½
[Branch of the "Connecticut Bank," Bridgeport.]

Conn. River Banking Co. Hartford,.......... do
[Wm. H. Imlay, Pres., Edwin Spencer, Cash.]

Danbury Bank, Danbury,...................... do
[S. Tweedy, Pres., A. Seeley, Cash.]
2's, engraved by Durand & Co—the genuine is engraved by Toppan, Carpenter & Co.
3's, description same as the above 2s.
5's, imitation of genuine threes—vig. drovers with cattle and sheep. The die work around the " 5 " is very coarse.
5s & 10s, vig. shipping, warehouses, &c.—not like genuine.

Derby Bank,................................Worthless

East Haddam Bank, East Haddam,........... ½
[E. A. Bulkley, Pres., T. C. Bordman Cash.]
5's, lett. C—vig. ship under sail—genuine has no ship.
5s, vig. a female, "five" on the right, a cow on the left.
5s, vig. a lady, spinning wheel,&c. a lady at the bottom.

Eagle Bank, New-Haven,................Worthless

Exchange Bank, Hartford,..................... ½
100s, altered from twos, vig. two females supporting a shield with various devices, one female has a sickle.
[Roderick Terrey, Pres., Elisha Colt, Cash.]
3's and 5's, altered from 1's.
5's, lett. C ; R. Terry, pres. Elisha Colt, cash. This is a poor imitation, very poorly engraved.
10's, altered from 1's, vig. State House. The words "Ten dollars" cover a part of the Cash's. signature.
10's, various dates, vig. a female seated and a man ploughing in the distance ; left end a ship with ful sail ; right, a marine view—engraving coarse.

Fairfield County Bank, Norwalk .... do
[A. E. Beard, Pres., T. Warner, Jr., Cash.]
1s, let. B, vig. railcars, buildings, &c. different dates.
5's, lett. E. pay E. Hawley, April 17 & Sept. 1, 1828.
5's, letter L, Sept. 1, dated at Norwalk, 1828. No bills, letter I, have been issued since Feb. 1, 1827.
10's, new plate—altered from smaller notes—the genine 10s have a floating female for a vig. and the goddess of liberty on the left margin.
10's and 20's, altered from 2's—old plate.

Farmers' & Mechanics' Bk., Hartford,...... do
[H. Goodwin, 2d, Pres., W. T. Hooker, Cash.]
1's, altered ; vig. reapers, agricultural implements, a dog, &c.
5's, altered, vig. reapers, farm-house and barn. W. Adams, Cash., H. H. Ellis, Pres.
10's, altered from 1s—vig. female, cows, &c.
5's, 10's, 20's, 50's and 100's, altered from the Farmers' & Mechanics' Bank. Burlington, Wisconsin Terr'y. Burton & Gurley engravers.

Hartford Bank, Hartford,..................... do
[D. F. Robinson, Pres., H. A. Perkins, Cash.]
2's, let. C., H. Burr, Cash., Terry, President. Both names appear to be the same hand writing.
3's, pay to D. Wilkinson, at the Merchants' Bank, N. Y., dated May 1, 1817.
3's, letter H. pay B. Hendricks, July 1, 1823.
3's, Jan. 1, 1820, Burr, Cash. Cardwell, Pres.
5's, lett. C., pay C. Day, Sept. 1, 1839, Perkins, cash., Trumbull, Pres. Vignette, whaling ships, and crew in small boat. Larger than genuine bill.
5's, letter C. Sept. 1, 1839, Perkins, Cash.
5's, lett. E. Jan. 1,1825, Horace Bent, Cash., instead of Horace Burr.
5's, lett. E. pay C. Corlis, & some E. H. Valentine, July 23, 1837. Others Jan. 1, 1828. Others April 29, 1827.
5's, lett. B. Jan., 1836, Rawdon, Wright & Co., N.Y., and Wrawdon, Clark & Co., Albany, engravers.
10s, vig. Indian, dog & dead stag—TEN on left end.
10's, lett. B. pay to T. Adams, Jan. 1, 1821.
10's, lett. B. pay to D. " Ilkinson, Aug. 1, 1839
10's, lett. B. pay to D. Wilkinson, Jan. 1, 1824.
50's, altered from 2s of same Bank.
100's altered from 1's of the same Bank

Iron Bank, Falls Village,...................... do
[Wm. H. Walton. Pres., R. M. S. Pease, Cash.]

Jewett City Bank, Jewett City,................ do
[David Smith, Pres. John Johnson, Cash.]
3's, let. A. variously filled up. Vignette, a female and sheaf of grain. Appearance bad.

Mechanics' Bank, New-Haven,................ do
[John Fitch, Pres., John W. Fitch, Cash.]
3s, vig. a man holding a globe, a farmer, oxen, &c.
5's, altered, signed Homer, cns., Warren, pres.
10's, altered from 1's, pay H. White, d fferent dates, the ink of the figure "10" & "X" are darker than the other parts of the bill. Well done.
10's, altered from 1's, 2's and 3's; well done.
20's, lett. C. pay D. Bacon, Jan. 1, 1828 and 1829.
20's, lett. C. pay to Wm. Lee, Oct. 3, 1828.

Merchants' Bank, Norwich,..................... do
[Wm. Williams, Pres., J. W. White, Cash.]
3s, three figures on the left end, and two agricultural views on the right. It is an altered bill. Look close.
3's, vig. a man with a scroll, and a figure 3 in the centre and on the left end.
5's, lett. C., July 5, 1841. Wm. Williams, Pres. W. White, Cash. Very Well done.

Meriden Bank, Meriden,........................ ½
[W. Booth, Pres., J. A. Butler, Cash.
3's, 5's, & 10's. altered. "Citizens' Bank" extracted and "Meriden Bank" printed on.

Middlesex County Bank, Middletown .... do
[C. R. Sebor, Pres., Wm. S. Camp, Cash.]
2's & 3's, altered—Samuel Russel, pres., E. Lacy, cash. Dated August 1, 1839.
2's, altered ; on the right reapers and dog, girl with a basket on her arm, and bundle on her head.
5's, let. in German, vig. cattle, a tree & steam engine. Counterfeit signatures.
10's, altered from 1's, easily detected.

Middletown Bank, Middletown,............... do
[J. H. Watkinson, Pres., F. L. Glenson, Cash.]
1's, OLD PLATE, lett. D. Jan. 1, 1817.
5s, vig. female with a child in her arms—and they read "Bank of Middletown"
10's, altered from 1's ; vignette of true ones. a female figure ; true 10's, vessels at sea.
10's, payable at the Mechanics' Bank, N. Y., May 1, 1817, others May 1, 1819.

Mystic Bank, Mystic,........................... do
[Elisha Faxon, Pres., Geo. W. Noyes, 2d, Cash.]
3's, let. B. engraving very coarse—vig. a female. The genuine has no female vignette.
5's, engraving coarse and signing poor, but likely to pass unless closely examined.

New-Haven Bank, New-Haven,................ do
[Hervey Sandford, Pres., A. Townsend, Jr., Cash.]
☞ All denominations, from the genuine plates, with counterfeit signatures and spurious filling up—refuse all the old notes. The bank is issuing bills from new plates, which are distinguished from the old notes by having a circular die representing the " First Sabbath in Quinnipiac, 1638."

New-Haven County Bank, N. Haven .... do
[H. Hotchkiss, Pres., R. Burritt, Cash.]
10's, altered from 5's, well done.
10's, altered from 2's. Easily detected.

New-London Bank, New-London.............. do
[J. B. Gurley, Pres., E. F. Dutton, Cash.]
1's, lett. B. pay to E. Chappell, (name engraved.)
3's, lett. A. June 1, 1836, pay to E. Chappell.
5's, lett. D. Nov. 1, 1825.
10's, lett. C. pay to J. Jones, July 7, 1823.

Norwich Bank, Norwich,....................... do
[C. Johnson, Pres., F. Johnson, Cash.]
5's, altered from 1s—well calculated to deceive.
5's, May 1, 1834, pay Lathrop, F. C. Working, cash.

Phœnix Bank, Hartford,....................... do
[Geo. Beach, Pres., John L. Bunce, Cash.]
2's, lett. G, engraving coarse and faint, paper flimsy.
2's, lett. D, pay David Porter, Jan. 1, 1818, filling up engraved.
2s, vig. female, eagle & shield—beehive, spade, &c. at the bottom—spelt " Payt " with a large B—genuine has n small b.
3's, lett. B. pay to H. Hendricks, July 1, 1823.
5's, lett. B. Oct. 17, 1838, J. Alden, cash., at this time J. J. Bunce was cash.—has " Paeson." for President.
5's, Oct. 4, 1837, Jos. Alden, Cash., H. Wells, Pres.
5's, dated and pay. at Litchfield, Aug. 1, 1831.
5's, lett. F. Oct. 1, 1821, pay to Bower.
10's, altered from 1's ; vig. a female with a sickle ; " TEN " defective.
10's, lett. A., Feb. 1, 1822. Pay Sol Porter.
10's, lett. B. May 1, 1828.
20's, altered from 2's : hold to the light.
20's, altered from 5's—vig. a female, in a car drawn by Cupid—Lafayette on the left and a figure of Justice on the right side of the vignette.

Phenix Branch Bank, Litchfield.............. do
[............., G. F. Davis, Cash.]

Quinebaug Bank, Norwich,..................... do
[S. C. Morgan, Pres., D. L. Trumbull, Jr., Cash.]
5's, vig. an eagle. The engraving and signing very bad—filling up quite bad.
10's, vig. a ship in a square frame. "Norwich" is spelt " Norwigh."

Stamford Bank, Stamford...................... do
[J. W. Leeds, Pres., Saml. R. Satterlee, Cash.]
5's, let. B vig. a shin and a person ; portrait on the right, female reaper on the left. Signatures engraved and pale, (in the genuine they are black,) filling up is stiff and coarse; in the genuine it is in a good hand.
5's, let. A. vig. Neptune & a female, in a car drawn by sea horse s. Signing bad
10's, vig. an eagle ; head of Washington on left end. The bank never issued any thing like this.

Stonington Bank, Stonington,................... ½
[Ephraim Williams, Pres., Francis Amy, Cash.]
3's, Nov. 5, 1822, lett. A. pay to W. R. Palmer.
5's, Nov. 4, 1822. Vignette coarse and light.
5's, in imitation of NEW PLATE, payable at the Merchants' Bank, N. Y. bust in the left margin.
10's, the vig. is on the upper right corner. The engravers' names, under the President's name, run up, instead of parallel with the lines. Letter C.

Thames Bank, Norwich,....................... do
[Edward Whiting, Pres., L. Brewer, Cash.]
5's, vig. a female holding a child.
20's, altered from 1s, "twenty dollars" in German text, stamped on the body of the note.

Thompson Bank, Thompson,................... ½
  [J. B. Gay, Cash.)
  5's, lett. B. March 1, 1839. Figure 5 larger than the true; appearance dark.

Tolland County Bank, Tolland,................ do
  [J. H. Brockway, Pres., Jona. R. Flynt, Cash.]
  5's, new plate, lett. D. Vignette, Cupids encircling the figure 5. Flint, Cash., Stearnes, Pres.

Union Bank, New-London,.................. do
  [J. Starr, Pres., J. C. Sistare, Cash.]
  1's, July 1, 1821, lett. G. pay to F. Swift.
  5's, Jan. 1, 1818, lett. C. pay to J. Maniere.
  5's, July 1, 1824, lett. C. pay to F. Swift.
  10's, altered from twos.

Whaling Bank, New-London,................. do
  [P. C. Turner, Pres., J. C. Douglass, Cash.
  2's, vig. a woman and anchor, engraving bad.
  5's, vig. female holding a scroll, rail cars in the distance.
  5's, May 1, 1840. Vignette a ship under full sail.
  5's, vig. wharf and rail cars, engraving pale.
  10's, vig. " Mercury " & a ship ; female on the right, denomination on the left ; Harris & Senly engravers.

Windham Bank, Windham,................... do
  [J. Baldwin, Pres., S. Bingham, Cash.]
  2's, vig. a female with a sickle on the figure 2 ; filling up and signing in the same hand writing.
  5's, lett. B. vig. a ship and female, signing and filling up in the same handwriting.

Windham County Bank, Brooklyn,........... do
  [J. Eaton, Pres., Adams White; Cash.]
  5's, lett. A. pay to G. Cobb, Feb. 2, 1823.
  5's, lett. A. A. pay. to H. Smith, Jan. 15, 1827.
  5's, lett. A, pay A. Stone. 1824.

NEW-YORK CITY.

The (F) means free, and (S) safety fund.

Agency & Exchange Bank,............... worthless

American Exch. Bank, 50 Wall st........(F.) par
  [D. Leavitt, Pres., John J. Fisk, Cash.]
  3's, altered from ones—hold them to the light.
  5s, altered from ones.
  5's, lett. D, various dates, J. J. Fisk, cash. D. Hadden, V. pres, the engraving is very coarse.

Bank of America, 46 Wall st..............(S.) par
  [Geo. Newbold, Pres., James Punnett, Cash.]
  3's, lett. D. pay to E. Duer, dated June 1, 1827.
  5's, lett. A. dated June 4, 1837,
  5's, lett. A. pay C. Day, dated June 1, 1833, signed D. Thompson, Cash., J. Taylor, Pres.
  5's, lett. D. pay to P. A. Jay, dated Jan. 1, 1820.
  5's, lett. D. pay C. Clark ; others, C. Cuyler, Jan, 4,1820.
  5's, pay to C. Graham, Sept. 3, 1823.
  5's, lett. A. May 5, 1834, (in some the date is omitted) pay S. Whitney—D. Thompson, Cash., Geo. Newbold, Pres. On the left hand margin the words " Printed by C. P. Harrison, N. Y." are NOT in the genuine notes with the signatures of the above officers.
  5's, lett. A. dated May 28, 1834, pay P. Crary. otherwise the same as above.

Bank of Commerce, 32 Wall st........ . . . . (F.) par
  [John A. Stevens, Pres., Geo. Curtis, Cash.]
  5's, lett. A. pay C. Crook, Jan. 8, 1845, John J. Stevens, pres., Geo. Curtis, cash. "Countersigned and registered," on the back. No. 1234.
  5's, engraving coarse, signatures bad. The genuine have Rawdon, Wright, Hatch & Co., immediately under the Pres. name, the count have not.
  10's, vig. an Indian, trees behind him & cars before

Bank of New-York, 48 Wall st............(S.) par
  [John Oothout, Pres., A. P. Halsey, Cash.]
  1's, lett. A. pay to J. Seymour, dated July 4th, 1840. Paper thin, ink of the signatures pale blue.
  5s, altered from ones.
  5's, lett. A. pay S. Randall, June 4, 1837, G. A. Worth, cash., Thos. Bloodgood, pres. Officers of City Bank.
  5's, lett. A. pay John H. Hicks, dated April 9, 1836, A. P. Halsey, Cash., Cornelius Hyer, Pres.
  5's, lett. A. pay R. Benson, Jan. 7;h, 1835, Cornelius Hyer, Pres., A. P. Halsey, Cashier.
  5's, lett. D. pay to C. Stone or bearer, Jan. 4th, 1825.
  5's, lett. B. dated Feb. 1st, 1833, Cor. Heyer, Pres., A. P. Halsey, Cash., pay to G. S. Robbins.
  5's, lett. B ; 1st Dec. 1829, pay to R. Vacick, signed Cornelius Hyer, Cashier, Ch. Wilkes. President
  5's, lett. A. pay L. Hill, dated 9th May, 1833, signed A. P. Halsey, Cash., Conis. Heyer, Pres.
  10's, altered from 1's, vig an engraving of the Bank, on one end an infant figure, on the other justice.

50's, let. A between the officers' names—vig. a floating female holding a shield, supported by an eagle—"FIFTY" extending entirely across the left margin—signing bad—light appearance.
100's, let. A between the officers' names—vig. a flying female, accompanied by a miniature female and a child—a large "C" each side of the vig. in a die about the diameter of a dollar—light appearance.

Bank of the State of N. Y;, 30 Wall st.....(S.) par
  [C. W. Lawrence, Pres., R. Withers, Cash.]
  ☞ Beware of the notes of the State Bank of N. Y. at Buffalo : Buffalo scratched out.
  5's, lett. D., May 21, 1841, filling up and signatures bad. Engraving poor. Paper flimsy.
  10's, altered from 1's. Observe that the final S of the words TEN DOLLARS is awkwardly inserted
  20's, altered from twos. Hold them to the light.

Bowery Bank, 173 Bowery........(F.).......... par
  [D. W. Townsend, Pres., Nat. G. Bradford, Cash.]

Butchers' & Drov. Bk., 122 Bowery,......(S.) par
  [Jacob Aims, Pres. Benedict Lewis, jr., Cash.]
  1's, alt'r'd from a broken bank. Hold it to the light.
  4's. No genuine fours in circulation.
  5's, lett. C. July 1, 1839. Bull's head on the left.
  10's, altered from ones and twos.
  10's, vig. a steamboat, "Fulton" on the wheel-house—"TEN" across the right end. Not like the genuine.
  20's, lett. B. vig. cattle under a tree, rail cars in distance denomination on both ends—have as engravers, Rawdon, Wright, Hatch & Co.—signing poor and stiff.

Chartered Bank,............................worthless

Chemical Bank, 216 Broadway,..........(F.) pa
  [J. Q. Jones Pres., J. B. Desdoity, Cash.]
  3s, vig. an eagle on a rock—figure " 3 " in each corner.
  3's, altered from Post Notes of the North River Banking Co. ; let. A ; Feb. 22, 1840 Vignette, a ship.
  3's, let E. old plate. A. Craig. cash, John Mason, pres.
  3's, pay G. Post or bearer, March 5, 1830.
  5's, let. C. pay Ph. Embury, & some W. T. McCoun, Nov. 25, 1830 ; A. Craiy, Cash., B. F. Melick. Pres.
  5's, let. C. Jan. 2,1850, pay G. Tucker; A. Craig. cash. B. P. Melick. pres. Paper light, a close imitation.
  5's, letter A. dated March 14, 1841, pay S. Johnson ; W. Williams, Cash., and A. Bummell. Pres.
  5's, lett. A. pay G. Tucker, dated Aug. 1, 1838. J Q. Jones. Cashier, John Mason, Pres.
  5's, altered from ones, old plate.
  10's, altered from 1's, by pasting an X over the 1 and stamping Ten Dollars over One Dollar.
  20's, altered from ones.
  50's, altered from ones ; very likely to deceive.
  50's, altered from 5's ; vig. a floating female ; the goddess of liberty on the left margin. The bank ha no 50's of this description.
  100's, spurious, letter A. April 5, 1543—signed J. L. Jones, cash., Isaac Jones, jr., prest.
  1000's, a large note—an inch longer and ¾ of an inch wider than bank notes generally. The bank has no 1000's out.

City Trust & Banking Co.,................... fraud

City Bank, 52 Wall st.....................(S.) par
  [G. A. Worth, Pres., Robert Strong, Cash.]
  2's, dated Feb. 20, 1827, lett. G. signed G. A. Worth, Cash., Isaac Wright, Pres. Others, letter K.
  5's, lets. B. b. in German. pay E. Hall Oct. 1, 1838, No. 466, G. A. Worth cash., Danl. Wright, pres. Paper white & thin ; engrs. by Draper, Underwood. Bald & Spencer.

Clinton Bank, New-York,.................(Closed) 50

Commercial Bank, New-York.........(Closed) do

Del. & Hud. Canal Co. cor. Wm. & Pine sts. (S,) par
  [John Wurts, Pres., J. H. Williams, Cash.]
  3's, let. D. pay to J. Platt, Sept. 1, 1832, signed J. H. Williams, Cash., John Wurts, Pres.
  3's, let D. pay to I. Jones, Nov. 5, 1832, signed J. H. Williams, Cash., John Wurts, Pres.
  3's, lett. A. Jan. 5, 1839, signed J. H. Williams. cash. John Wurts, pres.
  5's & 10's, altered from 1's, vig. a water-god in a recumbent posture—"3" in "Dollar", is smaller than the other letters. Can be discovered if held up to the light.
  5's, altered from 1's, let. A, May P. Hone, Feb. 6, 1826.
  10, lett. A. pay W. Ward, Sept. 1835.
  10's, admirably executed. They are a little shorter, and appear lighter than the genuine bills
  10's, lett. B. vig. Mercury, and a ship in the distance. Oct. 5, 1835. Paper flimsy.
  10's, lett. B. vig. Oct. 5, 1835, pay Rob'. Dyson ; J. H. Williams, Treas'r., John Wurts pres.—engraving well done.
  20's, altered from 9's.
  50's, altered from 5's—" FIFTY " inserted in place of the word " Five "—the former word being also smaller than the word dollars, with which it should correspond.

NEW-YORK CITY.

Exchange Bank, (J., Barker's,).............worthless
Franklin Bank,............................worthless
Franklin Manufacturing Co.................worthless

Fulton Bank, cor. Fulton & Pearl sts........(S.) par
 [John Adams, Pres., Wm. J. Lane, Cash.]
 5's, let. B, Aug. 1, 1831, pay Jos. Foulke. D. Thompson, Cash. Head on right margin defective.
 5's, lett. D. pay Silas Holmes, dated March 1, 1831, D. Thompson, Cash., John Adams, Pres.
 5's, lett. B. pay Amos Palmer, July 4, 1820, engrav'd by Durand & Wright—vig. is paler than usual, paper thin.
 5's, let. B. pay John Fleming, Feb. 5, 1831, D. Thompson, cash., John Adams, pres.
 10's, altered from good 2s, by pasting parts together.
 10's, altered from 1s; new plate.
 10's, let. A. in each end at top; Jan. 9, 1837, pay F Lovett; Jon (instead of John) Adams, Pres., W. J. Lane Cash.; the latter is well executed. Female figure at top in a reclining posture, holding a cap of liberty.
 20's, altered from threes.
 50's, altered from 3's, well done. The 50 is stamped over the 3 in the corners of the bill. ☞ Beware of Derby Bank notes payable at this bank.

Greenwich Bank, 402 Hudson st..........(S.) par
 [B. F. Wheelwright, Pres., Wm. Hawes, Cash.]
 1's & 2's, of the true plate. The President's name Satterlee, is spelt with but one l, Saterlee.
 3's, pay "to bearer," June 17th, 1841. Vignette a spread eagle. Engraving coarse and paper poor.
 5's, altered from 1's—hold them to the light.
 5's, vignette, agricultural scene. The genuine has Justice, and a lion's head.
 5's, altered from the post note plate of the North River Banking Co. Signed Schermerhorn. Pres.
 10's, alt'd from 2's—genuine has Washington on the left end, & "TEN DOLLARS" is in perpendicular letters.
 10's, altered, vig. the signing the declaration of independence. The genuine has an Indian, eagle, &c.
 10's, alter'd from 1's—name of the bank is printed on the top of the bill; In the genuine through the centre.
 20's, altered from 2's. Vignette a sloop under sail, and a female figure with a handful of wheat.
 100's, altered from some broken bank.

Globe Bank, New-York,....................... fraud

Hudson River Bank, New-York,.............. fraud

Lafayette Bank, New-York,.................Closed

Leather Manuf. Bank, 45 William st.....(S.) par
 [F. C. Tucker, Pres., Eb. Platt, Cash.]
 5's, vignette, a female. In the distance an agricultural scene. Not an imitation of the genuine.
 10's, alte'd from 1s—genuine have a small steamboat between the cash. & pres. names—the altered have not.
 10's, altered from Marble Manuf. Co., N. Y., Geo. L. Pride, cash. pay H. Hoosack, or order, H. Dennis, presidcot, endorsed.
 20's, particulars unknown.
 1,000's, lett. A., pay W. Goodsan, or bearer, 30d. after date, F. W. Edmonds, Cash., F. C. Tucker, Pres. Altered from some broken bk. post note.

Lumber Association,......................worthless

Manhattan Company, 40 Wall st.......(S.) par
 [C. O. Halstead, Pres., J. M. Morrison, Cash.]
 ☞ This bank has not issued notes since July, 1843, and its genuine notes are almost all in. There are, however, great many old counterfeits afloat.

Manhattan Exchange Bank,...............worthless

Manhattan Association,....?..............worthless

Marble Manufacturing Co.,................worthless

Mechanics' Banking Co.,..................worthless

Mechanics' Exchange Co.,.................worthless

Mech. Banking Assoc., 38 Wall st........(F.) par
 [Fred. Pentz, Pres., John H. Cornell, Cash.]
 3's & 5's, altered from 1s & 2s—altered by pasting figures over the original—bold them to the light.
 10's, altered from ones.
 20's, altered from 3's.

Mechanics' Bank, 33 Wall st.............(S.) par
 [S. Knapp, Pres., Francis W. Edmonds, Cash.]
 3's, altered from the "Derby Bank," Derby, Conn, a broken institution.
 5's, letter A., pay J. J. Astor, David Edmonds, Cash., Thos. D. Brown, Pres. Vig. a female & ship building.
 5's, altered from 1's, well executed. The word FIVE has been pasted across one end of the bill.

5's, lett. D. pay D. Bethune, dated May 4, 1828.
5's, let. D. pay to P. Sharpe; others to A. Van Nest, July 1, 1828.
10's, good imitat'on of genuine, payable to P. Henry, R. Irving, and others. Filling up rather good—the signature of F. W. Edwards is not done with the ease and elegance of the original. Paper poor.
10's, altered from 2's. The word "TEN" is printed much blacker than the rest of the note; well done.
20's, dated July 5, 1835, pay F. Hart, Fleming, pres. Baldwin, Cash.; others, lett. C. pay to S. Jaudon.
20's, altered from 3's. Very well executed.
50's, let. C. pay J. J. Astor, May 13, 1835—easily detected by the signatures. Also, some pay F. Cooper, dated April 12, 1833, H. Baldwin, Cash.

Mech. & Traders' Bk., 370 Grand st........(S.) par
 [John Clapp, Pres., E. D. Brown, Cash.]
 3's, let. C. Dec. 14, 1838, pay H. Hill or bearer—has "secured" by pledge of public stocks and real estate." Jas. W. Smith, Register. The back of the bill is plain.
 10's, altered from 5s—vig. blacksmith two females.
 20's, altered from 2's. The vignette is the genuine 20's is over the signature of the Cashier, and in the altered notes near the other end of the bill.

Merchants' Bank, 42 Wall st............(S.) par
 [John J. Palmer, Pres., O. J. Cammann, Cash.]
 2's, signed M. Clark, Cash., A. S. Stevens, President. There are no true bills with these signatures. Altered from Merchants Banking Co.
 3's, let. F. Jan. 1, 1834—"T" in 'to pay the,' not crossed.
 2's, lett. B. signed Walter Mead, Cash., Lynde Catlin. Pres., dated Nov. 1, 1823.
 2's, lett. A. dated Sept. 4, 1824, Vroom, Cash., Watson, Pres. No such president.
 2's, let. A. pay bearer, Nov. 1, 1825, J. G. Brown, pres.
 2's, lett. B. pay to bearer, Nov. 1, 1824, May 1, 1825. Others, March 1, 1826; also let. C. of same date.
 3's, vig. ship under full sail. Lynde Callen, pres.
 3's, Feb. 4, 1832—paper flimsy; vig. faint & coarse.
 5's, let. B. Feb. 1, 1842, O. Hammann, cash. John J. Palmer pres., genuine O. J. Cammann cash.—filling up and signing bad—good lithograph imitation.
 5's, lett. K. pay bearer, dated March 4, 1831. Walter Mead, Cash, Lynde Catlin, Pres.; No. 3221.
 5's, let. F. pay D. Wells, March 1, 1826. Others, pay to R. L. Lord, June 27, 1826.—Pay to J. Monroe, July 4, 1826.—Pay to D. Banks, July 8, 1826. This bank has never issued notes of any denomination whatever payable to Wells, Fleming, Lord, Blake, Monroe or Banks.

5's, No. 4719, pay J. Heard, April 1, 1836, purports to be engraved by N. B. & C. Durand, Wright & Co. The impression is like the genuine bill, but light and coarse.
5's, lett. E. pay B. S. Colt, dated March 1, 1826.
50's, vig. a steamboat, a ship in full sail and a pilot boat in the distance; below, rail car with locomotive.
100's, altered—true bill has O. J. Cammann, Cash. The counterfeit is signed O. J. "Hammann.

Merchants' Exch. Bk. 173 Greenwich st.....(S.) par
 [Jas. Van Ostrand, Pres., Wm. H. Johnson, Cash.]
 10's, lett. B. altered from 2's, dated March 1, 1841, signed W. H. Johnson, Cash., Peter Stagg, President.
 10's, lett. B. pay Thomas Wilson, March 21, 1840, W. M. Vermilye, Cash., Peter Stagg, Pres.—vig. a large steamboat. Purporting to be engraved by Rawdon, Wright, Hatch & Co., across the right end of the bill.
 20's, altered from 1's and 2's.
 20's, altered from 3's—detected by it having a single figure of Mercury in the centre, like the genuine 3's.
 1000's, ¼ an inch wider & ¼ inch longer than genuine.

National Bank, 36 Wall st.................(S.) par
 [James Galatin, Pres., F. Dobbs, Cash.]
 3's, let. A; vig. an eagle, and a man rising from the water; signing and filling up bad; engraving coarse.
 5's, read "the National Bank promises," &c. the genuine read "the National New-York promises," &c.
 5's, lett. D. May 16, 1837, pay to S. Grosvenor. Engraving coarsely done. Signatures engraved and ink. ed over. The filling up appear to be all in one hand.
 10's, vig. malt figure and eagle, Washington on the right end; some have coat of arms on the left, others the denomination, or head of. Washington.
 10's, altered from 5's. The 5's have for a vig. on the upper part of the bill, a small eagle, enclosed in a circle, around which appears the word "Five" several times.
 20's, altered from ones.

New-York Dry Dock Company,........(S.) par
 (Corner of Avenue D and Tenth street.)
 [George Hawley, Pres.,
 1's, genuine plates, false signatures. Rob't White, Cashier, E. Weeks, Prest.
 2's, let. C; pay O. Helms, Jan. 4, 1833—poor.
 10's and 20's, altered from 1's and 2's, very well done. Discovered by holding to the light.
 1000's, a large bill—good engraving. The bank has no thousands out.

New-York Exchange Bank,................ fraud

NEW-YORK STATE.

N. Y. State Stock Security B.,............(F.) par
[L. Bonnefoux, President,]
☞ *The notes are secured by N.Y. State stocks.*

The notes of this Bank are redeemed at par at 64 Wall st.
10s, altered from 2s, principal vig. has but one female, the genuine 10 has two females.

North River Banking Co.,............... fraud

New-York Loan Co.,.................... worthless

North River Bank, 175 Greenwich st.......(F.) par
[Nathaniel Weed, Pres., Aaron B. Hays, Cash.]
1's, lett. B. pay to C. Ainslee, dated Sept. 1, 1840. Paper spotted and uneven.
5's, altered from 5's of the North River Banking Co. by erasing the syllable ING and by the abbreviation Co. Vignette, an Indian figure. Signed Leonard Dodge, Cash., M. R. Schermerhorn, Pres.
5's, lets. D.—they at first appeared signed L. Kip, but now have the full name. LEONARD KIP, Cash.
5's, lets. B. b. June 1, 1830, pay to J. Hall, & others to J's. Kent; John Stebbins, Cash., Leonard Kip, Pres.
5's, lets. D. d. Oct. 4, 1830, pay to T. Brooks, No. 103. President's name is signed L. KIP, instead of Leonard Kip; the former signature in the genuine notes is confined to 1's, 2's and 3's, the latter to 5's and upwards.
5's, lets. B. b. dated Jan 1, 1828, John Stebbins, cash. Leonard Kip, pres.
10's, altered from one's, vig. a ship, date "1608" in the back ground; the vig. of the genuine 10's is the coat of arms of the State.
10's, altered from 2's—genuine have figures of commerce & manufactures, with their emblems; in the centre, betw'n them, a medallion of the Arms of the state.
20's, altered from 2's—vig. of genuine is a female in a sitting posture—a steamboat and sloop at a distance.

Phenix Bank, 43 Wall st...............(S.) par
[Thos. Tilleston, Pres., N. G. Ogden, Cash.]
2's, let. C. pay J. S. Crary, various dates. The vig. of the true bill is at the TOP—the bad one at the BOTTOM.
5 s, coarse lithog.—paper poor—signing bad.
5's, lets. D. D. J. Boggs, pres., D. J. Green, cash. President's name well done, filling up bad.
10's, altered from 1's, easily detected by noticing that it reads "TEN DOLLAR." the S omitted.
10's, let. B. April 1.1822, Ross, cash. Low. pres.
10's, spurious, let. B. pay C. Chandler, Jan. 1, 1824, signed Chas. French, Cash., Nath. Amy, Pres.
10's, lett. B. pay Joseph Grinnell, Nov. 2, 8126.
50's, the spread eagle is over "Phenix Bank,"—the eagle on the genuine 50 is at the left end.
500's, lett. B. pay Rufus King. good imitation

Seventh Ward Bank, 234 Pearl st.........(S.) par
[............., Pres., A. S. Fraser, Cash.]
5's, lett. A., pay to Hy. Clay. D. Lawrence, Pres.
H. Hanson, Cash. Well executed.
5's, lett. A. altered from 1's. The margin of the bill, with figure 1, torn off.
10's, let. A., counterfeit, vig. signing declaration of independence. H. Hanson, cash., Dan. Lawrence, pres.
10's, altered from 1's and 2's. Easily detected.
10's, altered from broken Tenth Ward Bank.
20's, altered. "Seventh Ward Bank," on the frauds is in one line—on the genuine it is divided by the vign'te.
50's, altered from two's. On the genuine two's "Seventh Ward Bank" is printed over the vignette; on the genuine 50's the vignette is on top.

Tradesmen's Bank, 177 Chatham st.......(S.) par
[W. H. Falls, Pres., Richard Berry Cash.]

☞ Beware of Checks on this Bank, purporting to be drawn by the Utica Insurance Co.
5's, altered from ones. Old plate.
5's, old plate "Five" stamp'd on in large red letters.
5's, lett. E., W. H. Falls, Cash., Preserved Fish, pres. Paper light, engraving coarse.
5's, lett. D. pay L. Seymour, dated June 2d, 1835, M. H. Falls. Cash., Preserved Fish, Pres.
10's, vignettes at the ends—purports to be engraved by Durand, Perkins & Co. N. Y. Countersigned on the back.— Engraving calculated to deceive, but filling up & signing is poorly done. Some have TEN in red letters, & some not.
10's, description same as the above, but has no letter.
10's, altered from ones—hold them to the light; the words "ten dollars" defective.
20's, lett. A., No. 1359, pay Dan'l Cooke. Vignette, a blacksmith at his anvil. On one end a countryman with cows, on the other rail road car.

Tenth Ward Bank, New-York,.............. fraud

Union Bank, 34 Wall st..............(S.) par
[F. Deming, Pres., D. Ebbets, Jr., Cash.]

☞ The genuine 1's & 2's of this bank are made payable to BEARER, all nigher amounts payable (in writing) to individuals.

1s, name of Daniel Ebbets, cashier, is spelt with two "tt"
1's, lett. H. July 4, 1839, Daniel. Ebbets, Cash., Wm. Howard. Pres. Lenev & Rollinson, engravers.
3s, very old plate, rather blurred; vig. a female, with a ship in the distance.
3's, altered from ones—hold them to the light.
3's, S. D. Day, Cash., N. Bishop, Pres. No such bills ever issued.
5's, A. W. Lawrence, Cash., R. McCarty, Pres.
5's, signed Alfd. Cotrell, Cash., lt. McCarty, Pres.
The Bank has never had such officers.
5's, let. D. pay J. Platt, July 1, 1820. Paper yellower than the true notes—name of the President engraved.
5's, let. I. pay W. Browne, June 17, 1838, Daniel Ebbets, Jr. cash., Wm. Howard, Pres—coarse engraving.
5's, lett. pay W. Bowne, dated Jan. 1, 1829.
5's, lett. E. payable to E. Troop, dated Jan. 1, 1830. Vignette pale, and engraving coarse.
5's, lett. I. pay to R. Barnes, June 4, 1830.
10's, altered from ones. Vignette of the 1's, a female figure on the lower margin
20's, altered trom ones.
20's, Edmonds, one of the engravers, is spelt "Edmona," otherwise it is a good counterfeit. Others, spelt "Edmonds." dated Sept. 1, 1841, Deming, president.
50's, altered from 1s: has the letter L each side of the vignette; the genuine 50's have no L.
50's, altered. A. supposed altered from the "Union Bank, Montreal," Dec. 10, 1840, pay to T. S. Howland, Dan'l. Ebbets, Jr., Cash., J. Deming, Prest
100's, altered from ones—the genuine read "the Union Bank promises to pay" the altered note reads "the Union Bank WILL pay," &c.
100's count'f. Vignette, a rail road and cars. Vignette of the genuine 100's a goddess and eagle

Washington Bank,........................ broke

Wool Growers' Bank,.................... Closed

NEW-YORK STATE.

Agricultural Bank, Herkimer,...........(F.) 1
[J. B. Dygert, Pres., P. F. Bellinger, Cash.]
1s, vig. a man, child, ship, &c.; female on the right. Imitation of genuine.
2's, altered, vig. female and sheaf of wheat.
3's, altered, the word TROIS on each end; vig. a female with a scythe, rake, spade, &c.
3's, not countersigned. "HERKIMER" stamph'd on.
5s, imitation of true bill—four females, two lions, &c.—a vessel in the distance—a dog between the officers names.

Albany City Bk, Albany,........(S.)....(100's *par*) - ¼
[Erastus Corning, Pres., Watts Sherman, Cash.]
2s, vig. female, cattle, &c.: " DEUX " on the upper left corner; and "deux piastres" along the upper margin.
5s, imitation of genuine; engraving coarse; left end printed in black ink—genuine is in blue.
20's, altered from ones

Albany Exchange Bank, Albany,.........(F.) par
[George W. Stanton, Pres., Noah Lee, Cash.]
1's, vig. female & child, a close imitation of genuine; engraved (coarsely) by Hall, Packard & Cushman, Albany.
1's, description same as the twos below, with one "J" in the centre of the bill—"Exchange" in large letters near the top, the genuine is engraved by Rawdon, Wright & Hatch, and notes of all denominations are the same as other free banks.
3's, the same as 2's above, excepting "III" in the centre.
5's, the same as above, with a large V in centre.
10s, altered from ones.

Amenia Bank, Leedsville,...............(F.) 1
[J. D. Hunt, Banker.]

☞ This is a new bank, and its notes are secured wholly by New-York State stocks.
3s, imitation of genuine: engrav. coarse, paper poor.
3's, altered from ones—the genuine 3's have two floating females for vig—the 1's have no dots.
5's, altered from 1s: hold them to the light.
10's, altered from ones. No tens out.
20s, altered from threes. No genuine twenties out.

American Bank, Mayville,...............(F.) do

Atlantic Bank, Brooklyn,..............(S.) par
[D. Embury, Pres., J. S. Doughty, Cash.]
2's, let. A, Draper, Toppen. Longacre & Co. engravers—Rawdon, Wright & Hatch, engraved the genuine.
5's, let. D. pay J. Sheldon; paper coarse & flimsy; engraving poor; filling up & signing done bunglingly.
5's, altered from 1's. The figure 5, and the words, "Five Dollars," are pasted on.
10's, lett. A. altered from ones,—vig. shipping, &c. arms of state on the left and—signed by the register.

Atlas Bank of New-York, Clymer,...(F.),.broke 30
[Ira F. Gleason, President.]

☞ The comptroller has taken as security for the notes of this bank, one bond and mortgage for $65,000. This certainly is not ample security. The "Real Estate" on the note is so engraved as not to be discovered without difficulty.

NEW-YORK STATE.

Ballston Spa Bank, Ballston,..............(F.) ¼
[James M. Cook, Pres., Isaac Fowler, Cash.]
1's, imitation of genuine, engraving coarse, the lettering of "Ballston Spa Bank" blurred and very coarse.

Bank of Albany,......(S.)....(50's & 100's par) do
[J. H. Teneyck, Pres., Jellis Winne, Jr. Cash.]
3's, lett. A. May 1, 1838; filled up with blue ink.
5's, let. C, old plate, pay C. Clay. E. Olcott, cash,r.
5's, altered from counterfeits on Bank of St. Albans.
5's, let. D. filled up with blue ink, J. Winnie, cash., also in blue ink.
5's, lett. A. pay to J. Q. Adams, dated July 2, 1844. An entire different plate from genuine.
5's, W.H. Wynkoop, cash., J. P. Van Ness, pres. The Bank never had a President or Cashier of these names.
5's, lett. A. pay G. Winne or bearer, Nov. 1, 1836, Barent Bleecker, pres., J. Winne, cash. Another, also let. A. pay to A. Van. Vechten or bearer, date not filled in.
5's, lett. H. The dle on the upper left hands larger than the genuine, and the top of the P, in the word Pre-silent, runs up in that die, whereas in the genuine it does not quite touch it.
5's, "Five Dollars" s pasted over One Dollar.

Bank of Albion,..............................(F.) 1
[R. S. Burrows, Pres., L. Burrows Cash.]
5's, vig. four human figures, one holding a key in one hand and a globe in the other--indistinct impression.

Bank of Attica, Buffalo, (formerly Attica,)...(F.) do
[G. B. Rich, Pres., A. J. Rich, Cash.]
1's, 2's, & 3's, signed S. D. Day & N. Bishop. The genuine are all signed by G. B. Rich, Pres.
5s, let. B; counterfeit; filling up and signing is poor.
10s, altered from ones. Hold them to the light.

Bank of Auburn, Auburn,..............(S.) do
[Cornelius Cuyler, Pres., J. S. Seymour, Cash.]
1's, lett. B. Oct. 10, 1839—pay B. Starke, old plate.
1's, 2's & 5's, S. Stiles, Sherman & Smith, N.Y. engra.
1's, letter A., Septem. 1, 1842, pay S. Bond, E. Beach, Pres. Seymour, Cash. Others lett. B.
1's, lett. B., E. Canfield, dated Sept. 22, 1831. J. S. Seymour, Cash., and E. Bewell, Pres.
1's, let. A. Oct. 17, 1839, the A. is not crossed—pay B. Cole, J. S. Seymour, cash., Daniel Kellogg, pres. Paper thick, stiff, and of a pale cast. Others lett. B.
2's, lett. A., pay D. Davis, E. Beach, Pres., Seymour, Cash., Stiles, Sherman & Smith, engravers. Genuine engraved by Draper, Underwood & Co.
5's, let. A., vig. a female sit'ting, a scroll in her hand; a locomotive in the distance, pay J. Jones, June 29, 1841.
5's, let. A. Nov. 6, 1826, pay J.Q. Adams; others Aug. 3, 1832, I. S. Seymour, cash D. Kellogg, pres.
5's, lett. A. April 1, 1817; others Oct. 8, 1817; others July 1, 1841, Cash. and Pres. same as above.
5's, lett. A. pay to B. Read or bearer, Aug. 1, 1841, J. Seymour, Cash, Daniel Kellogg, Pres. Engraved by S. Stiles, Sherman & Smith, N.Y.
10's, let. A. pay Cuyler. Dec. 2, 1817, Mumford, pres.

Bank of Bainbridge, Chenango co.....(F).... do
[L. Bigelow, Pres,]

Bank of Brockport,...............(Closed) 25
5's, let. B. pay Jas. Clark, Sep. 1, 1840, (sam. John C. Nichols, Cash., E. B. Holmes, V. Pre.

Bank of Buffalo,..............(Closed,) 50
[Ira A. Blossom, of Buffalo, Receiver.]

Bank of Cayuga Lake, Ithaca......(F.)..broke 15
☞ The notes of this bank are secured wholly by N. Y. Stoc.

Bank of Central New York, Utica,......(S.) 1
[A. Thomas, Pres., T. O. Grannis, Cash.]
1's, vig. a man, child, ship, &c.; female on the right.
5's, pay D. Cushman, Jan. 2, 1841, T.O. Grannie, cash. A. Thomas, Pres. The lettering very irregular.

Bank of Chenango, Norwich,..............(S.) do
[I. Wilcox, Pres., Walter M. Conkey, Cash.]
3's, lett. 1. pay A. Hunter, dated Oct. 7, 1838.
3's, let. I. pay A. Hunter, Norwich, Oct 7, 1838, Abraham Raimond, Cash., Ira Wilcox, Pres., both names in one handwriting. Some have Walter M. Conkey, cash.
5's, lett. D. pay to E. Williams, May 2, 1825.
5's, pay C. Clark, May 4, 1832, Jas. Birtjsnli, cash, Ira Wilcox, Pres. Others lett. B. pay N. Ely, July 4, 1832.
5's, lett. E. Norwich, Oct. 4, 1835, pay M. Barber, James Phedeall, cash. Ira Wilcox pres —vig. coarse—ce'light.
5's, lett. B. April, 1855, pay H. Kellogg.
5's, lett. T. pay H. Stone, Norwich, Nov. 10, 1857 James Phidell, Cash., Ira Wilcox. Pres.
5's, lett. T. pay H. Maxwell, signed H. Hill, Cash., Ira Willcox, Pres.
5's, let. T. payable to Lester Nyr. dated Dec. 4, 1836, James Phideall. Cash., Ira Wilcox, Pres.

Bank of Columbia, Hudson,................worthless

Bank of Corning,......................(F.) 1
[H. W. Bostwick, Pres., L. Mallory, Cash.]
1's, vig. a lady resting on an arm of flowers—a steamboat on the right end.
5's, a very coarse lithograph.

Bank of Dansville, Dansville,..............(F.) 1
[Lester Bradner, Pres., L. C. Woodruff. Cash.]
3's, the genuine notes are marked on the end "S u-red by pledge of pubblic stocks and real estate;" the spurious thus, "Secured by pledge of publicstock."
5s, vig a group of females—a child at their feet—coarse.

Bank of Genesee, Batavia,..............(S,) do
[P. L. Tracy, Pres., J. E. Robinson, Cash.]
1's, pay A. C. Stevens. Sep. 1833, J. S. Canson, cash., T. Carey, Pres. The vignettes entirely different from the genuine—paper light and thin.
5's, let. A., June 10, 1838. T. Can, Pres. The genuine are signed T. Carey, Pres.

Bank of Geneva..........................(S.) do
[C. A. Cook, Pres., Wm. E. Sill, Cash.]
1's, lett. A. pay H. R. Troup, dated July 1. 1819, signed J. Rees, Cash., H. Dwight, Pres.
2's, lett. D. paper thin and oily, signatures poorly executed, particularly that of a C. A. Cook.
4's, lett. A. pay to R. Troup, dated Oct. 1, 1818
5's, spurious. The bank has never issued 3s.
5's, let-er L. stereotype plate, Feb. 1, 1832, pay to J. Ward, as J. Walter, C. A. Cook, Cash., W. E. Sill, vicepres. Also. C. A. Cook, Cash., H. Dwight, pres.
5's, let. A. March 1, 1818 ; some 1825, pay Jonas Platt.
5's, lett. A. and F.; both letters imperfect for want of the cross.
5's, lett. R. dated March 1, 1826, pay to Jonas Platt, signed J. Rees, Cash., H. Dwight, Pres.
10's, pay J. Day, dated Jan. 1, 1818, J. Rees, Cash., H. Dwight, Pres.
10's, lett. A. pay to R. Troup, Jan. 1, 1824.

Bank of Ithaca,..............................(S.) do
[Wm. Randall, Pres., W. B. Douglas, Cash.]
☞ All bills payable at Buffalo are frauds.
1's, let. B, pay James Monroe, March 5, 1832, others to H. Clay, July, 1837, with different names for officers.
3's, lett. H. dated May 4, 1840, pay B. Bell, H. Heneger, Cash., L. Seymour, Pres. Pale.
5's, lett. F. dated Jan. 10, 1836, pay J. S. Mott, signed T. P. St. John. Cash., A. St. John, Pres.
5's, vig. head of Franklin; Luther Gore, pres. A. St. John, cash—genuine has check plate on the back.
5's, pay B. Drake, March 15, 1830, Luther Gore pres, A. St. John, cash. Extremely well executed. No. 2501.
5's, let. B—A. St. John, cash. Daniel Bates, pres, pay H, Panfully, March 1, 1835. The heads of Washington and Franklin are miserable imitations.
5's, lett. F. June 12, 1836, pay Wm. Randall,—A. St. John, Cash, Daniel Bates, Pres. General appearance light, engraving fair, and likely to deceive. Also, some pay H. Panfully, lett. F. dated May 2, 1836.
10s, altered from twos—easily detected.

Bank of Kinderhook,......................(F.) par
[J. P. Beckman, Pres., Covington Guion, Cash.]
10s, vig. a shield, globe, eagle & two females—ends 1½ inches wide with TEN at top & bottom & a head betwen Steamboat between the president and cashier's names.

Bank of Lansingburgh..............(S.) ¼
[J. s. Fake, Pres., P. M. Corbin, Cash.]
5's, lower part of the "g" in Lansingburgh touches the nose of the horse—various dates.
5's, old plate, let. B, vig. a female & agricultural implements—A.C. Lansing, Pr. Jas. Reid, Ch.—letter "S" in "Bank of Lansingburgh" larger than the other letters.
5's, new plate, let. A—vig. horses, cattle & sheep, covered bridge in the distance—E. W. Walbridge, pres. P.M. Corbin, rash—the signatures appear to be engraved—the small words "five dollars" on the top and bottom margins are indistinct & defective—the dies around the figure "5" are badly executed.
5s. let. A. has Draper, Tappan & Co. as engravers—coarse.
3s. let. B. the female in vig. has but three fingers—the FIVE DOLLARS, on the margin, is rather crooked.

Bank of Lake Erie, Buffalo,.............(F.)........ 1
[D. N. Barney, Pres., T. M. Janes, Cash.]

Bank of Lowville,......................(F.) do
[I. W. Bostwick, Pres., Jas. L. Leonard, Cash.]
3's, vig. female in a circle; 'DOL' at top, instead of dollars.

Bank of Lyons, Lyons...............(Closed) 10
5's, counterfeit, vig. cattle and rail cars. Filling up and appearance bad.
5's, let. R. A. R. Wesson, cash., G. Corning pres.
5's, let. F. vignette cattle and sheep standing under a tree, railroad car in the distance.
10's, letter C. vig. Perry's victory. In the genuine note it is an agricultural picture.

Bank of Monroe, Rochester,..............(S.) 1
[J. K. Livingston, Pres., Ralph Lester, Cash.]
☞ Beware of counterfeits on the above bank, signed R. R. Gibson, Pres., R. S. Pomeroy, Cash.
1's, 2's, 3's & 5's, altered from broken Bank of Monroe, Michigan,—Michigan was at the top, and has been torn off.
2's, letter A. dated June 17, 1839 signed P. Robson, Pres. S. C. Miller, Cash.; filling up very bad
10's, altered from ones—well done.

Bank of Newburgh......................(S.) pat
[John Chambers, Pres., George M. Kerr, Cash.]
10s, vig. a female, eagle, &c., a small eagle between the officers names. Diff rent from the genuine.
10's, let. R. "SAFETY," is spelt without the "F."
10s, vig. female and eagle—TEN across the left end.

NEW-YORK STATE. 15

Bank of Niagara, Buffalo,..................worthless

Bank of New Rochelle,...................(F.) 1
3's, altered from 1's—the genuine threes have a floating female for a vignette.
10's, altered from one s and twos.

Bank of Orange County, Goshen,.........(S.) ½
[A. S. Murray, Pres., Thos. T. Reeve, Cash.]
2s, let. B. b. pay I. Jennings, July 1, 1826.
3's, letts. A. a. pay T. Decker, April 1, 1832; others, of same letter and date, pay to J. Wheat.
3's, letts. A.a. Aug. 3, 1830, Jn. Smith, pres., H. Seward, cash., pay E. Jansen. Others, Oct. 3, 1831.
3's, letts. A. a. dated April 4, 1831, pay to S. Ward. Vignette pale, signatures stiff.
5's, letts. A.a. Jan. 1, 1855, pay S. Townsend, A. S. Murray, cash., J. W. Smith, V. Pres. Paper pale yellow.
5's, letts. C. c. pay C. Lindsay, March 4, 1827; others, o H. Williams, June 10, 1827; none of these, the old plate, were ever signed by Seward, Cash. or Smith, V. Pres.
10's, letts. A. a. pay to D. Maffit, dated July 1, 1829. Paper of a deeper yellow than the genuine.
10's, lett. A. dated Nov. 3, 1835, pay to S. Townsend A. S. Murray, Cash., G. D. Wickham. Pres.
10s, good imitation, name of Geo. D. Wicham, pres. is in a steady firm hand—the genuine is is an unsteady liand.

Bank of Olean, Olean..................closed

Bank of Orleans, Albion,.................(S.) 1
[A. Ward, Pres., T. S. Clark, Cash.]
3s, vig. a country scene, female with sheaf of wheat, &c.
5's, pay to Wm. C. Detch, & signed F. Clark, Cash., Alex. Ward, Pres. Vignette, Jackson.
20's, altered from 3's; vignete at each end is covered over, as also the two figure 3's at the top.

Bank of Owego,...................(S.) do
[Jonathan Platt, Pres., James Wright, Cash.]
1's, vig. a steamboat; an Indian on the left end, and a painter with a scroll and brush on the right.
2s, let. G, engraving coarse, filling rather good.
3's, vig. a female riding a dragon—genuine has an eagle for a vig. The die-work around the figure 2 is only about half an inch in diameter, on the genuineit is an inch in diameter.
2's, letter A., altered from the broken Globe Bank, signed S. B. Day.
5's, let. C—the M in " demand" is irregular, and the last "d" has the appearnnce of o l.
10's, various dates, paper coarse and thick.
10's, let. C—on the right end is an Indian with a dog and a prostrate deer; on the left, a female.

Bank of Plattsburgh,...................worthless

Bank of Poughkeepsie,..................(S.) par
[Tims. L. Davis, Pres., Reuben North, Cash.]
5's, A Harris, Cash., W. J. Hill, Pres. On left margin an Indian; on the right, a steamboat.

Bank of Rochester,...................(S.) 1
[J. Seymour, Pres., H. S. Fairchild, Cash.]
3's, vig. steamboat; registered on the back by S. R. W. Hasbrouck. No boat on the genuine.
10's, letts. A. a. July 1, 1835, pay C. Tucker, signed J. Seymour, Cash., T. Bushnell, Pres.
5's, coarsely executed—genuine have the heads of Washington and Fraklin; on the counterfeit they look like Tom Benton in a thunder storm.
10's, let. B. pay W. Whitney, Oct. 1, 1835; well done. Others, let. B. Sept. 1, 1835, a J. Jones. Others, to J. Hills: which name is not on the genu.
10's, let. C. July 4, 1834, pay E. Peck. J. Seymour, Ch. T. Bushnell, Pr.—close imitation, and likely to deceive.
10's, lett. B. pay J. Childs, dated Aug. 1, 1835, J. C. Moore, Cash., T. Bushnell, Pres.
10's, letts. A. a. dated Dec. 4, 1835, pay to Jno. Sage, signed J. Seymour, Cash., T. Bushnell, Pres.

Bank of Rome,...................(S.) do
[John Stryker, Pres., G. R. Thomas, Cash.]
☞ Spurious bills, of various denominations; they are altered from the Bank of Romeo, Michigan.
1's, lett. C., pay W. C. Bouck, engraving coarse.
3's, lett. A. Sept. 4, 1840, John Wood, cash. John Striker, pres.—note shorter than the genuine. Also, some Henry A. Foster, prest.
5's, Indian viewing a town in the distance—cattle and sheep on the left end. Altered from a Michigan concern.

Bank of Salina,...................(S.) do
[D. Monroe, Pres., M. W. Bennett, Cash.]
5's, count., lett. D., Feb. 1, 1841. Rather coarse.

Bank of Saratoga Springs,.......(F.) ½
[Thos. J. Marvin, Pres , Jas. M. Marvin, Cash.]

Bank of Silver Creek,...................(F.) 1
[Geo. W. Tew., Pres., C. C. Swift. Cash.]
5s, imitation of genuine, vig. 4 female- in a group, much blurred ; filling up in boy's hand ; engraving poor.

Bank of Syracuse,...................(F.) do
[J. Wilkinson, Pres., Horace White , Cash.]
5's, engravers' names are printed "Rawdon, Wright, Hatch," N. Y. instead of "Rawdon, Wright & Hatch,"

Bank of Troy,...........(S.)....(50's & 100's par) ¾
[Nathan Dauchy, Pres., John Paine, Cash.]
1's, lett. B., May 1, 1838, pay P. Ford. Appear to be lithographed. A good imitation.
2's, lett. A. dated Nov. 6, 1829.
3's, the "a" in Bank looks like "w."
5's, let. A. vig. a female—"five" on the right and a cow on the left—registered on the back.
10's, lett. T. pay B. Joslin, dated Jan. 3, 1829.
10's, lett. A. dated Oct. 1, 1838.
20's, let. A ; vig. locomotive and train of cars.

Bank of Utica,...................(S.) 1
[Thomas Walker, Pres., W. B. Welles, Cash.]
3's, lett. Z. Jan. 4, 1830, not all filled up.—HOUSE, in "Banking-House," is spelt HONSE. Vignette coarse.
3's, lett. D. P. Hunt, cash. H. Huntington, pres.
3's, lett. M. dated in 1832, " Renewed Charter."
3's, lett. E. pay to D. W. Clinton, engraved—W. O. Welles, Cash., H. Huntington, Pres.
5's, lett. K. old English, pay to Dewitt Clinton, Aug. 4, 1835, H. Huntington, Pres.; vignette coarse.
5's, let. f. pay to D. W. Clinton, (engraved.)
5's, lett. W. dated Utica, Jan. 4, 1830.
5's, lett. B. pay to B. Drake or bearer.
5's, altered from 1's. Exceedingly well done; vignette of the true 1's is State Arms
5's, let. F. & let. H. Jan. 4, 1830, H. Huntington, pres., M. Hunt, cash. Well executed. Vignette rather coarse, the sheep's head resembles that of a horse.
5's, letter I. dated Jan. 1830, pay to D. W. Clinton. Vignette coarse—well calculated to deceive.
10's, let. A. Utica, Jan. 4, 1830, pay D. W. Clinton, at Canandaigua—vig. coarse, otherwise a close imitation.
20's, Jan. 4, 1839 ; others, lett. F. ; some 1833

Bank of Vernon,...................(F.) do
[John J. Knox, Pres., T. F. Hand , Cash.)
3's, an alteration; no resemblance to the genuine.
5's, let. A. dated 8, 1840, pay Wm. Bentley, S. Case, Ch. John J. Knox, Pr.—vignette, two Indians, & a steamboat in the distance. Back plain ; the genuine is red.
10's, let. A. ; not countersigned. Genuine notes are engraved by Rawdon, Wright & Hatch, N. Y.
20's, fraud, not registered nor countersigned.
50's, let. A.—vig. a sailor seated on a bale of goods, with a flag in his left hand ; on the left end is a full length figure of liberty. Not countersigned.

Bank of Watertown,...................(F.) do
[W. Ives, Pres., W. H. Angell, Cash.]
3s, a coarse imitation of the genuine.

Bank of Waterville,...................(F.) do
[J. Candee. Pres., D. B. Goodwin, Cash.]
5's, let. C, registered in red ink by G. Hanford.

Bank of Whitehall,...................(S.) do
[Wm. A. Moore, Pres., W. H. Palmer, Cash.]
3's, altered from 1's of Hoboken Bank, N. J.; Bank of Whitehall stamped on on large letters across the top.
5's, spurious, altered from " Hoboke ; Banking and Grazing Co," "Bank of Whitehall," at the top of the notes instead of the centre.
10's, an alteration; "WHITEHALL, inserted.

Bank of Whitestown,...................(F.) do
[S. Newton Dexter, Pres., J. S. Thomas, Cash.]
1's, vig. a man, child, ship, &c.; female to the right, very poorly engraved. An imitation of the genuine.

Black River Bank, Watertown,.........(F.) do
[L. Paddock, Pres., H. G. Gilbert. Cash.]
5s, altered from ones—vig. a cow and a country girl.

Brooklyn Bank, Brooklyn,...........(S.) par
[W. J. Cornell, Pres., Abraham Halsey, Cash.]
5's, altered from a broken Michigan Bank.
10's, altered from 1's & 2's—hold them to the light.
3's, supposed to be altered from the broken Monroe Bank, Mich. Brotberton, Cash., Adams, Pres.

Broome County Bank, Binghampton......(S.) 1
[C. Strong, Pres., T. R. Morgan, Cash.]
1's, imitation of genuine; vig. a man, l orse, boy & girl —on the right a female without a mouth ; paper whitish.
3's, let. B. Nov. 5, 1830, and some Jan 10, 1832, pay P. Pine, & some to R. Boyd—paperislighter—vig. coarsely engraved, that of Hope much lighter; note s little shorter. There is a small space between the first line, on which the name is written to whom the bill is payable, and the top of the D in the word "Demand." The D in genuine covers the lines.
5's, lett. C. pay R. Boyd, of various dates.
5's, dated June 2, 1832, pay to J. L. Bowne, C Murdock, Cash., V. Whitney, V. Pres.
20's, altered from 1's; there are few 20's out.

Canal Bank, Albany,...................(S.) ½
[John K. Paige, Pres. Theodore Olcott, Cash.]
1s, an excellent imitation of the genuine—the only difference being in the quality of the engraving.
3s, lett. D, vig. a Grecian temple, counterfeit signatures, engraving coarsely done.
3's, lett. A. new plate; vig. goddess of Liberty, &c. Poor paper; filling up and signing bad.

NEW-YORK STATE.

3's, altered from the broken Globe Bank, N. Y., signed S. B. Day, Cash.
3's, let. A& some G, various dates—well done.
5's, counterfeit—let. E—D. Campell, register, filling up and signatures very bad.
10's, altered from ones—goddess of liberty on the left end—"TEN DOLLARS"slightly defective.
20's, altered from 3's.

Canal Bank of Lockport,.................(F.) 1
[William O. Brown, Pres., G. W. Rogers, Cash.]
5's, pay E. Hurd. Coarsely engraved, signatures bad.
5's. altered from ones.

Catskill Bank, Catskill,..................(S.) par
[Thos. B. Cook, Pres., H. Hill, Jr. Cash.]
2's, lett. B, dated Nov. 1, 1825, H. Hill, Jr. Cash
2's, let. A. (Nov. 1, 1827, engraved,) Paper whitish.
2's, letter B. Nov. 1, 1825, H. Hill, Jr. cash. Tho. B
Cooke, pres. New plate; date engraved, thick and yellow paper, engraving is coarse. K in CATTSKILL, in upper part of note, is below the other letters.
3's, vig. female, chest & abip; N. Quackenbush, register.
5's, lett. C. Nov. 1, 1828, pay C. Hopkins. Vignette, an Indian shooting a panther, very well done.
5's, lett. C. pay E. Powers, June 5, 1830—vig. Indian shooting a panther—face of Franklin particularly light.
5's, lett. C. pay to C. Hopkins, Nov. 1, 1829.
5's, let. A. Nov. 1, 1836—Carder, Durand, Austin & Edmonds, engravers—close imitation of genuine—engraving rather coarse—margins are broader—Cashier's name is a FAC SIMILE—President's is not so good.

Cayuga County Bank, Auburn,...........(S.) 1
[N. Beardsley, Pres., J. N. Starin, Cash.]
5's, lett. B. engraving coarse, vignette blurred, and the whole bill black and dirty
10s, lithograph imitation, let. A, July 1, 1843, pay A. G. Beardsley—this & the officers names are printed & traced.

Central Bank, Cherry Valley,............(S.) do
[D. H. Little, Pres., H. J. Olcott, Cash.]
1's, old plate, the engraving is coarse and indistinct, and paper poor.

Champlain Bank, Ellenburgh,..............(F.) do
[J. B. McLane, Pres., M. Hale, Cash.]
5s, altered from twos, vig. two females holding a shield.
20s, altered from twos, vig. two females holding a shield.

Chautauque Co., Bank, Jamestown,......(S.) do
[Saml. Barrett, Pres., Robert Newland, Cash.]
5's, let C.vig.an indian with a bow; registered on the back; cashier's name is Robt. Newland on the genuine; & "Rot. Newhunt" on the counterfeit. Engraving coarse.
5's, lett. D., pay C. Gilbert, Jan. 1, 1841. Filling up and signatures bad. A poor imitation.
10's, let. B. Jamestown, Dec. 4, 1836 pay S. Hurd—E. T. Foot, Pr., A. D. Putchin. instead of PATCHIN, Cb. Faper thick—others, Jan. 14, 1837, pay H. Pratt.
10s, let. A, pay C. Weed—Paper thin, engraving coarse. C. Tappan & Co.. engravers, Phila. and N.Y.
10's, lett. A. April 4, 1838, pay James Gray.
20's, altered from J's—vig. Is a group of cattle; the genuine has a heathen divinity, on the right, in a recumbent position, and on the left the figure of a horse.

Chemung Canal Bank, Elmira,............(S.) do
[Chas. Cook, Pres., John Arnot, Cash.]
5's, let. D., pay A. Bent. H. Maxwell, Cash., J. G. M'Javell, Pres. Poorly executed.
10s, imitation of genuine; vig. man emptying a vase; on the right, woman & eagle; horse's head betw'n John Arnot cash. & Charles Cook, pres—signing & countersigning bad.

Chester Bank, Chester,....................(F.) ½
[Jas. Wheeler, Pres., Alex. Wright. Cash.]
5's, vig. four female-, with globe, key, &c, a lion at their feet.

City Bank, Buffalo,........................(Closed.) —

Clinton Co. Bank, Plattsburgh..,.......(Closed,) 10
[H. K. Averill, Receiver, Plattsburg.]

Commercial Bank, Friendship,............(F.) 1
[Luther Stowell, Banker.]

Commercial Bank, Lockport,..............(F.) do
[S. P. Stokes, Banker.]

Commercial Bank, Troy,..................(F.) ½
[Stephen W. Dana, Pres., Fred. Leake. Cash.
☞ Bills of ALL denominations, on this bank, altered from broken Comm. Bank. Millington, Md.

Commercial Bank, Albany,................(S.) par
[J. Townsend Pres., James Taylor, Cash.]
☞ Bills of ALL denominations, on this bank, altered from broken Commercial Bank, Millington, Md.
1's, let. A. vig. several vessels under sail—appears pale.
1's, Townsend, Pres. Pale, and poor imitation.
1s, large "1" each side of vignette—appearance light.
3's, engraved by "Durrant & Co." from the spurious "Commercial Bank of Poultney," which has been altered to "Commercial Bank of Albany."
3's, let. A. J. Taylor cash, John Thomson, pres.
3's, appearance light, vig. ship at a wharf. and a small schooner with her sails alongside, a steamboat at a distance. On the left hand is an Indian seated on a rock.
5's, let. D. Dec. 20, 1837, pay on bearer, Seth Hastings, Pr., J. Taylor, Cash.—vig. a steamboat and two vessels. Purport to be engraved by Durand & Co., N. Y.

Commercial Bank, Buffalo,..........(Closed,) 10
[S. G. Austin, of Buffalo, Receiver.]
☞ The most of the genuine bills of this Bank have been redeemed, and those now in general circulation are mostly sp rious.

Commercial Bank, Rochester,............(F.) 1
[Asa Sprague, Pres., Geo. R. Clark, Cash.]
☞ Bills of ALL denominations, on this bank. altered from broken Commercial Bank, Millington. Md
5's, with red back—engraving coarse, the Register's name miserably done.
3's and 10's, altered. Engraving good, the names of the State, and the place where the bank purports to be located. stamped on by hand.

Commercial Bank of Oswego,........(Closed,) 10
[Thomas Beekman, of Kinderhook, Receiver.]
3s, vig. female figure, engraving faint and coarse.

Cuyler's Bank of Palmyra..............(F.) 1
[George W. Cuyler, Pres.. S. P. Seymour, Cash.]
☞ Notes secured wholly by N. Y. State Stocks.

Delaware Bank, Delhi,...................(F.) do
[H. D. Gould, Pres., J. W. Sherwood, Cash.]
5's, lithograph—well calculated to deceive.

Drovers' Bank, Olean,....................(F.) do
[G. W. Smith, Pres., John L. Haines, Cash.]
5's, let. G—vignette in female with a staff.
5s, vig. four females, lion, ship, globe, &c., engraving coarse.

Dutchess County Bk., Poughkeepsie,......(S.) par
2's, vig. a female with one arm extended; Fonda, Cashier, Swift, President. Paper light and coarse.
3's, let. A. June 1, 1836. The paper is of a yellowish tinge, thin and coarse. The whole execution, particularly the figures, is bad.
5's, vig. a female with scales, and a ship under full sail. Jas. R. Fonda, cashier, H. Swift, president.
10's, let. B., Alex. Forbes, V. Pres.—vignette, a ship at sea. paper thick, paper of genuine is thin.
10's, lett. D., pay L. Mason, and others H. A. Livingston. Paper thick and whiter than genuine.
10's, altered from 1's—bold them to the light.

Essex County Bank, Keeseville,............(S.) 1
[S. Arnold, Pres., A. Thompson, Cash.]
5's, vig. a female and agricultural implements, locomotive in distance—plough, grain, &c., between the signatures.
10s, lett. B, vig. a female and bird; TEN on the right end, counters gned by H. F. Flagg, paper whitish. N. Thompson, cashier, Silas Arnold, president.
10's, vig. a blacksmith shoeing a horse; Rawdon, Wright & Hatch, N.Y., engraved the genuine.
20's, coarsely engraved, lithograph appearance.

Exchange Bank, Buffalo,...................(F.) do
[R. Codd. Pres., A. Honliston, Cash.]
5s, altered, vig. female, anchor, &c., ship in the distance.
10's, altered from ones.

Exchange Bank, Lockport,................(F.) do
[Henry Harvey, Prest., W. T. Rogers, Cash.]
3s. vig. a female in a circle. Impression light.
3s; vig. two females and a portrait; has a human head between the signatures, genou e has an eagle.

Exch. Bank of Genesee, Alexander,.....:(F.) do
[Henry Martin, Pres., Heman Blodgett, Cash.]
5's, altered from 1's, by substituting the figure 5 and the word five for one.

Exchange Bank of Poughkeepsie,......worthless

Farmers' Bank, Troy,....................(S.) par
[J. Van Schoonhoven, Pres., Ph. Wells, Cash.]
1's, lett. E. pay to bearer, dated Nov. 4, 1822.
2's, very coarsely engraved.
3's, lett. B. Aug. 16, 1840, P. Wells, Cash. G. Corning, Pres. Paper very light, engraving well done and calculated to deceive.
5's left. F. pay to A. Eighth, Oct, 1, 1813.
5's, dated March 7, 1827, and some Oct. 7, 1822—lett. H. pay to G. S. Clute, J. C. Schoonhoven, Cash.
10's, Nov. 30, 1836, others 1837—steamboat between the officers' names, which is not in the genuine.
10's, these notes are engraved for the Farmers' Bank of Houston, Texas.
20's, vig. agricultural scene, female on the left, they rend "Farmers' Bank of Troy," &c.—the genuine read, "Farmers' Bank of THE CITY of Troy."

Farmers' Bank, Amsterdam,................(F.) 1
[C. Miller. Pres., N. P. Wells. Cash.]
1's, altered from a post note plate, vignette, a female with a sickle, not reg'd or countersigned.
1's, let. A. Aug. 1840, L. Johnson, cash, H. Brown, pres. Red back, paper thin. Washington on left end.
2's, drawn in form of Checks are frauds.
3's, let. B, Aug 2, 1840, L. Johnson, Ch., H. Brown, Pr.
5's, new emission, let. A. vig. a female with a sickle, C. Miller, pres. R. H. Palmer, cash.
20's, let. A; vig. a lady, cows, sheaf of grain, &c—on the eit a lady with a shield—at the bottom an Indian's head.

Farmers' Bank, Mina,......................(F.) do
[J. Relf, Pres,]

NEW-YORK STATE.   17

Farmers' Bank of Cattaraugus Co.,...... fraud
Farm. Bank of Penn Yan, Romulus,...... worthless
Farmers' & Drovers' Bank, Buffalo,......(D.)   2
　2's, there is a circle around the figure 2 in the genuine, the counterfeit has an octagon.
　5's, spurious—no genuine fives ever issued.

Farm. & Mech. Bank, Rochester,........(F.)   1
　[A. G. Smith, Pres., E. Huntington, Cash.]
　5s, not registered or countersign'd.'Rochester' stamp'd on.
　5's, let A, has the word "safety fund" on it, and the names of the officers of the Oneida Bank.
　10's, alterations,"Rochester"stamped on.
　20's, altered from a Michigan shinplaster; "Rochester," stamped on.

Farm. and Drov. Bank, Somers,........(F.) par
　[Horace Bailey, Pres., E. Howland, Cash.]
　2's, let. D ; counterfeit signatures

Farmers' Bank, Geneva,................(F.)   1
　5's, alter'd f'm a broken bank."Geneva" stamp'd on.
　10s, altered from 1s—vig. female, chi d, &c.

Far. & Mech. Bk. of Genesee, Batavia,....(F.) do
　[J. S. Ganson. Pres., J M Ganson, Cash.]
　☞ Beware of bills, purporting to be of this bank, altered from a broken bank of same name in Michigan.
　1's, vig. a man, child, ship, &c.; female on the right.
　3's, May 1, 1842, altered from the above bank, signed J. E. Robinson, Cash., P. L. Tracy, Pres.

Farm. Bank, Warwick, ...(Closed) 2

Farm. & Mech. Bank, Ogdensburgh.......(F.)   1
　[S. Gilbert, Pres., J. T. Vanderhoof, Cash.]
　2's, altered from ones.
　5's, let. B.—G. Handford, register—signing badly done.
　10s, altered from 2s; vig. female and agricultural impliments ; the genuine 10s have two females.

Farm. & Manuf. Bank, Poughkeepsie.....(S.) par
　[Wm. A. Davies, Pres., E. P. Benjamin, Cash.]

Farmers' Bank, Hudson,................(F.) par
　[Elihu Gifford, Pres., Henry Jenkins, Cash.]
　☞ Beware of 1's, 2's, 3's and 5's spurious. We have not yet obtained a good description of them.

Fort Plain Bank, Fort Plain,..........(F.)   1
　[J. Webster, Pres., Isaiah C. Babcock, Cash.]

Fort Stanwix Bank, Rome,............... do
　[............, Pres., David Utley, Cash.]

Franklin Bank, French Creek,..........(F.) do
　Wm. H. Jones, Banker.]

Franklin County Bank, Malone,........(F.) do
　[S. C. Wead, Pres., E. Stephens, Cash.]
　5's, altered from 1s, vig. in the centre a female supporting the 1—genuine has a large V and a female on the right end.
　10's, altered from 2s.
　20's, altered from 2s. The bank has no 20s out.

Genesee County Bank, Le Roy,.........(F.) do
　[John Lent, Pres., M. P. Lampson, Cash.]
　☞ All denominations of the broken B'k of Genesee, at Flint Rapids, Michigan, altered so as to read "Bank of Genesee County." Farmers over the vignette.

Greene Co. Bank, Catskill,.............worthless

Herkimer Co. Bank, Little Falls,......(S.) 1
　[Hy. P. Alexander, Pres., Albert G. Story, Cash.]
　5's, let. B. paper very poor, and filling up bad.

Henry Keep's Bank, ... do

Highland Bank, Newburgh,..............(S.) par
　[Geo. Cornwell, Pres., A. Post, Cash.]
　3's, vig. female and agricultural female. The words 'Highland' & 'Newburgh' stamp'd on.

Howard Trust & Bk Co., Troy,.....(Closing) —

Hudson River Bank, Hudson,..........(S.) par
　[Oliver Wiswall, Pres., Cary Murdock, Cash.]
　☞ Beware of notes on this bank dated in New-York; they are frauds.
　5's, altered from 1's—well done.
　10's, letter A., Thomas W. Haynes, Cash., Edw. Smith, Pres., they never signed the genuine.
　10's, let. C. various dates—vig. an Indian with his right hand erected—railroad cars in the distance.

Hungerford's Bank, Adams,............(F.) 1
　[S. D. Hungerford, Banker.]
　☞ The notes of this Bank are secured wholly by New-York State stocks.
　10's, altered from 1s—"8," in dollars, done with a pen.

James' Bk, (Saratoga Co.) Jamesville, (F.)..broke 30
　[J. W. James, Pres., A. D. Grinnell, Cash.]
　☞ Notes secured by real estate and Michigan stork.
　3's, engraving coarse, particularly the portrait of Mr. James at the bottom of the note.
　5's, signed by P. D. Prindle as register.
　5's, letter A. signed F. W. Huxford, register, J. W. James, Pres., A. D. Grinell, Cash.
　10's, altered from ones. The bank has no tens out

Jefferson County Bank, Watertown,......(S.) 1
　[N. M. Woodruff, Pres., O. V. Brainard, Cash.]
　2s, vig. a man emptying a bucket of water.
　2's, let. B, pay to D. Lee, vig. Vulcan, and a female with a shield on the left end.
　3's, lett. A., O. V. Brainard. Cash., O. Hungerford, Pres. Jan. 4, 1841. Paper milky white.
　5s, vig. a female, eagle and shield, with a 5 on each Paper of a purple cast. Durand & Co. engravers.
　5's, lett. F. Oct. 1, 1835, pay J. Ward—O. H. Brainard, Cash. Paper light and the engraving coarse.
　10's, let. A. Jan. 4, 1836, pay J. H. Whipple.
　50's, let. A. No. 67—Durand & Co. engravers.
　50's, vig. a floating female and bird; Durand & Co. engravers.
　100's, similar to the 50s above.

Kingston Bank, (Ulster Co.) Kingston,......(S.) par
　[J. S. Smith, Pres., Wm. F. Romer, Cash.]
　5's, J. C. Smith, cashier, E. Launsberry pres't,—"New-York Safety" not on a straight line. "Kingston Bank" coarsely done.
　5's, vignette, an agriculturalscence, cows, plough, &c.; the genuine has two females and an engle.
　5's, letts. M. D, pay to A. Harrison, Oct. 1, 1857. S. Smith, Cash., E. Lumsbuy, Pres.
　10's, vig. an Indian gazing at railroad cars. Romer, cash., Smith, pres.
　10's, altered from a broken bank; A. Howe, cash.

Kirkland Bank, Clinton,...............(F.) 1
　[A. G. Gridley, Pres.,]

Lewis County Bank, Martinsburgh,.....(S.) do
　[L W. Bostwick, Pres., R. L. Lyon, Cash.]
　3's, let. A. pay J. Jones, June 10, 1838, Stephen Leonard, V. Pres., C. L. Mather, Cash.
　5's, lett. A. Jan. 1, 1837. Filling up indistinct and miserable; engraving coarse
　50's, vig. canal lock, mills, field of grain with respers; arm and hammer between the officers' names.
　50's, let. A. vig. a barn and outhouses,—D. L. Lyon, pres. D. S. Hungerford, cash.

Livingston County Bank, Geneseo......(S.) do
　[Allen Ayrault, Pres., Ephraim Cone, Cash.]
　5's, altered from a broken bank ; between the president and cashier's names are these words · "realestate and personal property holden"—nothing of the kind on the genuine.
　10's, altered from 1s ; vig. a man ploughing with oxen.

Lockport Bank & Trust Co.,...........(F.) do
　[W. Hunt, Pres., G. W. Germain, Cash.]
　10s, altered from 1s ; vig. a female, child, vessel, &c.

Long Island Bank, Brooklyn,..........(S.) par
　[L. Lefferts, Pres., Geo. L. Sampson, Cash.]
　1's, the genuine have a man on horseback in the corner. the counterfeits have not.
　3's, vig. a man on a horse. Others have a lady.
　5's, altered from 1's. The 1's have a man on horseback, the genuine 5's have not.
　10's, altered from 1's & 2s—the genuine have a man sitting upon rocks, in the centre of the note.

Luther Wright's Bank, Oswego.........(F.) 1
　[L. Wright, Pres , S. H. Lathrop. Cash.]
　5's, counterfeit—engraving coarse, paper poor.
　10's altered from ones of this bank.

Madison County Bank, Cazenovia,......(S.) do
　[J. Ten Eyck, Pres., T. W. Seward, Cash.]
　2's, July 8, 1839, officers R. G. Spencer, A. M. Burt, Watsou, register—paper coarse and light.
　5's, vig. a man cradling, with a ship on the right; W Watsou, register—paper coarse and light.

McIntyre Bank, Adirondack, Essex co.,........ 1

Mech. & Far., Albany, (S.)......(50's & 100's par) do
　[T. W. Olcott, Pres., E. E. Kendrick, Cash.]
　5's, altered from 1's—closely done, new plate, dated May 1, 1823, signed B. Knower, Pres.

Merchants' Bank, Poughkeepsie.........(F.) par
　[M. J. Myers, Pres., J. H. Fonda. Cash.]
　☞ The circulating notes of this Bank are secured wholly by New-York State stocks.
　10's, different from the genuine ; vig. a female, eagle,&c. A small eagle between the names of the officers.

Merchants' Bank, Buffalo,.............(F.) 1
　[Miles Perry, Prer., J. L. Haines, Cash.]
　5s, altered from ones.

Merchants' Bank, Canandaigua,.........(F.) do
　[............, Pres., W. Blossom, Cash.]
　☞ Notes secured wholly by N. Y. state stocks.

Merchants' Bank, Ellery,..............(F.) do
　[O. Benedict, Pres., T. M. Leonard, Cash.]
　2s, altered from ones, vig. locomotive and cars.

Merch. and Farm. Bank, Carmel........(F.) do
　[S. Washburn, Pres., Edgar Washburn, Cash.]

Merch. & Farm. Bank, Ithaca,............(F.) 1
[T. S. Williams, Pres., J. B. Williams, Cash.]
3's, an alteration; this bank has no 3's out.
5's, altered—"Bank of Ithaca," shows the alteration. Vignette, a steamboat—two large "**5**" below.
10's & **20**'s, altered from a broken bank note. This bank has no 20's out. Its 10's have red backs.

Merch. & Mech. Bank., Troy,.............(S.) 3/8
[George Vail, Pres., Charles S. Douglas, Cash.]
1's, vig. woman & vase of flowers; woman on right steamboat on the left. Paper and engraving poor and heavy. Payable to bearer.

Mech. & Traders' Bank, Albany,..........worthless

Middletown Bank, Orange County,.........(F.) 3/8
[J. Davis, Pres., Wm. M. Graham, Cash.]
5s, vig. dark; cashier's name is spelt "Craham" instead of Graham. But the C can be easily altered to G.
5s, vig. 4 females, with globe, key, &c.—lion at their feet.

Middle District Bank, Poughkeepsie,......worthless

Mohawk Bank, Schenectady,...............(S.) 1/4
[J. I. De Graff, Pres., W. B. Walton, Cash.]
1's, vig. an Indian; registered on the back by H. H. Van Dyck; poor engraving.
3's, letts. M. m. dated Schenectady, Oct. 12, 1830, signed D. Boyd, Cash., D. Martin, Pres.
3's, letts. L. l. Schenectady, pay to bearer, May 12, 1832, D. Boyd, cash, D. Martin. pres.—old appearance, paper thin—vignette of the Indian coarsely engraved.
5's. Perry's victory is in the centre of the bill—on the right, an Indian, and on the left a lady.
10's, lett. C. pay to J. Case, Dec. 30, 1838, D. Boyd, Cash., D. Martin, Pres. Paper whiter, & the figure of the Indian much too small, compared with the genuine.

Mohawk Valley Bank, Mohawk Village,..(F.) 1
[Elias Root, Pres., F. E. Spinner, Cash.]
5's, counterfeit, old emission, and plate check, letter D. The bank has never issued fives letter D.

Montgomery Co. Bank, Johnstown,.........(S) do
[James W. Miller, Pres., Ed. Wells, Cash.]
1's, **3**'s, **5**'s & **10**'s, altered from a broken western bank.
3's, altered from a broken Michigan plate; vignette, reapers &c.—Washington on the right.
5's, let A in German text; vig. cattle, tree, and locomotive; female with corn on the right, two 5's on left—"countersigned and registered" on the back—D. Holt, register, in blue ink, paper thin.
5's, counterfeit, vignette, a reaper reclining on a sheaf of wheat, with sickle elevated, bull's head on left margin. The genuine has no bull's head.
10's, altered from the broken bank of Millington.

New-York State Bank, Albany,...........(S.) 1/4
[Rufus H. King, Pres., J. B. Plumb, Cash.]
1's, lett. E. pay to bearer, dated July 1 1829.
1's, letter E. Jan. 9, 1839, John T. Norton, Pres., R. Yates, Cash. Engraving and filling up poor.
1's, lett. E. Jan. 1, 1838, signed E. Olcott, Cash., John T. Norton, Pres.
3's, let. A. The engraving is very bad, particularly the female in the vignette.
5's, altered, Massachusetts coat of arms on the right side Has the names of Draper, Toppan & Co., as engravers.—"New" in New-York is spelt "Now"
5's, vig. images swinging in a wreath—very unlike the genuine.
10's, pay to order of Erastus Corning, V. Pres., but not endorsed, dated July 1, 1830.
20's, altered from twos.

New-York Stock Bank, Durham,..........(F.) 1
[Platt Adams, Pres., A. Marks, acting Cash.]
☞ *The notes of this bank are secured wholly by New-York State Stocks.*
5's, Lithograph, paper & filling up poor; the counterfeit has no commas in the engravers' names, and the engraving is coarse.
10's, altered from 2's—vignette a female and cattle; Washington on right end.
20's, altered from 1s and 2s—the bank never issued 20s

Northern Bank, Madrid,.......................(F.) do
[John Horton, Pres,   ]

Northern Canal Bank, North Granville,..(F.) do

Northern Exch. Bank, Brasher Falls,.(F.)..broke 15
[C. T. Hubbard, Pres., J. N. Hindale, Cash.]

Ogdensburgh Bank, Ogdensburgh,.......(S.) 1
[James Averill, Pres., John D. Judson, Cash.]
5's, let. B. pay S. Gilbert—D. C. Judson, cash., Turner, V. pres; whole appearance bad.

Oliver Lee & Co.'s Bank, Buffalo.........(F.) do
[I. T Hatch, Pres., F. H. Tows, Cash.]
5's, let. A—the figure "5" on right end poorly done—"Liberty" at the upper part of it is scarcely legible—has the appearance of a wood cut.

Oneida Bank, Utica,........................(S.) do
[A. Munson, Pres., B. B. Lansing, Cash.]
3's, vig. rail cars, &c.—genuine has a female.
3's, letter A. Oct. 21st, 1840, pay W. Bates; others, H. Lee, Dec. 25, 1840.
3's, lett. B. The words "New-York Safety Fund," are at the top of the bill.
3's, lett. A. paper thin & white—"New-York Safety Fund," is on the left end; genuine has it on the right.
5's, lett. C. dated Nov. 24, 1838, signed B. B. Lansing, Cash. A. A. Munson, Pres.

Oneida County Bank, Utica,................worthless

Onondaga County Bank, Syracuse,........(S.) 1
[Oliver Teall, Pres., Hamilton White, Cash.]
3's, vig. Syracuse House; filling up poorly done, engraving coarse; the filling up of the geunine is good.
3's, imitation of genuine plate, pay D. Dana, vig. and head of Dewitt Clinton coarse; Haml. White, cash. M. S. Marsh, pres. Likely to deceive.
3's, they have "Onondaga Bank." The genuine reads "Onondaga County Bank."
5's, vig. ship under sail—the genu. has no ship.
10's, good imitation of genuine; Haml. White, cash. M. S. Marsh, pres. Engraving coarse. Pa per light.
10's, let. A—faces are coarse and unnatural. Engraved by Rawdon, Clark & Co., Albany. Registered and countersigned.

Ontario Bank, Canandaigua,...............(S.) do
[John Greig, Pres., H. B. Gibson, Cash.]
3's, lett. A. pay to J. Bacon, Jan. 1, 1827.
5s, altered from ones—vig. a female sitting, with quiver, &c.
5's, lett. B. pay to N. W. Howell, Canandaigua, Oct. 1, 1835, H. B. Gibson, Cash., John Gray, Pres.

Ontario Bank, Branch, pay at Utica,....(S.) do
[A. B. Johnson, Pres. Thomas Rockwell. Cash.]
5's, lett. E. pay C. Jones, Utica, Aug. 1, 1836, A. B. Johnson, Pres., Thos. Rockwell, Cash.—paper thin,—impression coarse & pale. Some Jan. 1, 1834, No. 723, pay S. D. Childs, Also Jan. 1, 1834, No. 572.
5's, lett. F., in German text; payable at tee branch in Utica, B B under Pres.
5's, May 1, 1836, H. Rochewell. Ch., A. B. Johnson, Pr.
5's, let. E. July 1, 1836, signed A. B. Johnson, Pres., Th. Rockwell, Cash. Appearance Pale.

Oswego Bank, Oswego, (S.)............(Closed) 50
[Winding up, C. Stebbins, Receiver, Cazenovia.]
☞ There are no genuine bills of this bank in general circulation, those out are mostly spurious.

Otsego County Bank, Cooperstown,.......(S.) 1
[Robert Campbell, Pres., H. Scott, Cash.]
2s, vig. a female, impression light Proper signatures.
2's, letter D., pay to G. W. Strong, paper greasy. Others lett. X. pay F. Cooper, May 4, 1842.
5's, lithograph, well calculated to deceive.

Palmyra Bank, Wayne County,...........(F.) do
[Pliny Sexton, Pres., ... Cash.]

Patchin Bank, Buffalo,.....................(F.) do
[A. D. Patchin, Pres., Thad. W. Patchin, Cash.]
10's, altered from 1s, vig. female with sickle, grain, &c., locomotive in the distance.

Pine Plains Bank, Pine Plains,............(F.) do
[R. W. Bostwick, Pres., F. W. Davis, Cash.]

Powell Bank, Newburgh,...................(F.) pur
[Samuel Williams, Pres., T. C. Ring, Cash.]
5's, vig. same as genuine—engraving coarse.

Pratt Bank, Buffalo,..........................(F.) 1

Prattsville Bank, Prattsville,.............(F.) par
[Z. Pratt, Pres., J. Hopkins, Cash.]

Rochester Bank. Rochester,..............(F.) 1
[Freeman Clarke, Pres., P. W. Handy, Cash.]

Rochester City Bank, Rochester,..........(S.) do
[Thos. H. Rochester, Pres., C. T. Amsden, Cash.]
3s, a lithograph. Very bad looking.
3's, altered from ones—hold them to the light.
5's, lett. C., pay D. S. Gregory, June 1, 1842. General apprarnee blurred. Signatures bad.
5's, let. B.,—have "Rawdon, Wright, HATCH", N.Y. as engravers, instead of "Rawdon, Wright & Hatch."
20's, altered from 10's; hold them to the light.

Sackett's Harbor Bk...................(S.) do
[E. G. Merick, Pres., J. C. Dann, Cash.]
3's & **5**'s, vig. Mercury and a ship; a steamboat between the signatures. Blurred appearance.

Saratoga County Bank, Waterford,.......(S.) 1/4
[J. Knickerbocker, Pres., M. S. Scott, Cash.]
3's, vig. an eagle, ship, and a hogshead; registered on the back. Paper quite white.
10's, vig. ship under full sail, in a frame. Pay H. Stewart, which is engraved instead of written.

Security Bank, Huntsville.....................(F.) 1
☞ Notes secured by bond and mortgage in part.

Schenectady Bank, Schenectady,..........(S.) 1/2
[J. Cady, Pres., Wm. L. Goodrich, Cash.]
5's, lithographed—let. A. in German—vig. a spread eagle, countersigned on the back—Thos. Palmer, cash. Arch. Craig, pres't. Engraving and paper very poor
10's, let. A; vig. an Indian surprised at rail cars—two X's on each end; a vessel on the right, an Indian viewing rail cars on the left—a dog, key and safe at the bottom.
10's, vig. an Indian with hand up raised, and a bow by his side; the genuine have an Indian with his bow raised and bent, ready to discharge an arrow

Seneca County Bank, Waterloo...........(S.) 3/8
[David S. Skaats, Pres., W. V. J. Mercer, Cash.]
5's, the words "Seneca County Bank" in perpendicular letters, the genuine are slanting letters.
5's, altered, have "real estate and personal property holden," between the officers' names, which is not on he genuine bill.

NEW-JERSEY.

10's, let. G. vig an Indian with dogs, tomahawk and rifle. W. V. 1. Mercer, cash., D. B. Jones, pres.
20's, altered from a fraud; vig. a boy under a haycock and uralle; genuine has no such picture.
50's, lett. A—E. Swan, register, Wm. V. J. Mercer, cash. Prouty, pres. Various dates. Good engraving.

State Bank, Saugerties, ... (F.) .... broke 15
[R. N. Isaacs, Pres.,]
☞ Notes secured wholly by New York stocks.
5s, let. A, imitation of genuine—THE before STATE BANK, in black letter, in the genuine it is white block letter—after the letter A, the spurious has a full-point, the genuine has not signatures engraved—engraving rather dark.

State Bank of N. Y., Buffalo, ... (Closed) 75
Staten Island B'k, Port Richmond, ... (Closed) 50
St. Lawrence Bank, ... (Closed) 70

Steuben County Bank, Bath .... (S.) 1
[W. W. McCay, Pres., J. Magee, Cash.]
3's, lett. H. dated July 7, 1838, pay to P. Cook, vig. an ox, and view of a cottage—head of Washington on each end. Miserably engraved.
3's, let. I—head of Washington on the right, head of Franklin on the left end—impression pale.
3's, lett. I. pay to H. Clay, signed T. Taylor, Cash., Walter Smith, Pres., dated May 18, 1839.
5's, let. C. pay A. B. Johnson—countersigned by the register—Jan. 5, 1841. At this date there was no law requiring his signature. Others, let. C. vig. a singe & horses—lithograph—J. Mayer, cash., some John Mayer, cash.
10's, pay H. Smith, Foster, cash., Merritt, pres.

Suffolk County Bank, Sug-Harbor, ... (F.) do
[Wm. Adams, Pres., G. N. Adams, Cash.]
☞ Notes secured wholly by N. Y. State stocks.
5's, 10's & 20's, altered from ones and twos.

Tanners' Bank, Catskill .... (S.) par
[S. S. Day, Pres., F. Hill, Cash.]
3's, let. A. pay J. Platt; O. Day, pres., F. Hill, cash; vig. coarse, signing & filling up poor; others, let. C. pay S. Moore; the head of the eagle is not visible.
5's vig. goddess of liberty, an eagle, &c.; genuine have the Cattskill mountains, with tanners at work.

Tompkins County Bank, Ithaca .... (S.)
[Herman Camp, Pres., N. T. Williams, Cash.]
1's, let. B; vig. rail road cars; the houses have no windows or chimneys, in the genuine have.
2's, vig. eagle, shield, and goddess of liberty sitting —badly engraved. A female, ship, &c. on the right.
2's, altered; two females on the right end.
3's, altered; let. A; vig. man with a grain cradle.
5's, letter C. dated Nov. 1, 1838, S. A. Man, Cash., A. Camp, Pres. General appearance very dark.
5's, vig. a female holding a key; two females on the right margin, and one on the left.
10s, on the right is Liberty, a ship and the arms of the U. S. on the left is Justice with scales, a bale of goods, mechanics tools, &c.—"10" on each end. The signatures are in the same hand. Engraving poor—purporting to be by Durand, Perkins & Co—filling up and signatures in pale blue ink.
20's, altered; vig. a group of agricultural emblems; on the left end, Venus rising from the sea.

Troy City Bank, Troy, ... (S.) ½
[George B. Warren, Pres., Silas K. Stow, Cash.]
5s, poor engraving—vig. steamboat; cattle on left end.
5's, let. E. vig. a steamboat—railroad on the right; engraving good—it is a broken bank note altered.
5's, 10's and 20's, altered from the Tenth Ward Bank, N. Y., worthless. S. K. Stow, Cash.

Unadilla Bank, Unadilla .... (F.) 1
[A. B. Watson, Pres., C. J. Hays, Cash.]

Ulster County Bank, Kingston .... (S.) par
[C. Bruyn, Pres., J. S. Evans, Cash.]
5's, an imitation of the genuine, register's name lithographed. Appearance bad.

U. S. Exchange Co., N. Y., ... worthless

Warren County Bank, Johnsburg .... (F.) 1
[L. B. Barnes, Pres., W. W. Watson, Cash.]
5's, between the officers' names is a steamboat; the genuine has "secured by the pledge" &c.

Washington Co. Bank, Union Village, ... (F.) do
[Henry Holmes, Pres., E. Andrews, Cash.]
5s, vig. Perry's victory—registered & countersigned on the back—engraved by Mason and Taylor.
5s, vig. water scene—Washington & Webster on the ends.

Watervleit Bank, West Troy, ... (Closed) 10

Westchester County Bk., Peekskill, ... (S.) par
[P. Van Courtlandt, Pres., I. Seymour, Cash.]
5's, letter A., not an imitation of true bill; by close inspection the word "Otsego" is found in the vignette.

White's Bank, of Buffalo, ... (F.) 1
[Geo. C. White, Pres., Wm. Williams, Cash.]
5's, let. C. vig. three females, the countersigning and filling up is bad.

White Plains Bank, White Plains .... (F.) 1
[E. Crawford, Pres.,]
1's, has G. Crawford as pres. instead of C. Crawford—the A & D in Cadmus cash. do not join, in the genuine they do.
3's, altered from ones; the bank has no threes.

Wooster Sherman's Bk., Watertown ...... (F.) do
[W. Sherman, Pres., Chas. Burchard, Cash.]

Yates County Bank, Penn Yan, ... (S.) do
[Asa Cole, Pres., William M. Oliver, Cash.]
2's, let. A—head of Washington is very coarse, and the signing and filling up is not well done.

3's, let I—vig. very indistinct—Washington on the right and Franklin on the left. Appearance rather light.
3's, let. I. Oct. 2, 1838; N. B. Cook. cash., Asa Cole, pres; vig. an ox, and a hut in the distance.
Other signed T. Brown, cash., H. Dayton, pres.
3's, lett. I. Charles Penez, cash., Nathan Dixon, pres. Vignette as above—paper flimsy.
5's, altered from ones—hold them to the light.
5's, lithograph, well done, let. D, signing bad.
10's, vig. a female, cows, ploughs and sheaves of rain—engraved by Rawdon, Wright & Hatch.
20's, lett. a. vig. railroad, village in the distance; engraved by Danforth Bald Spencer & Hufty—this house never engraved 20s for the bank.

NEW-JERSEY.

☞ $1, $2 and $3 notes on the South Jersey banks, 1

Bank of New Brunswick .... worthless

Belvidere Bank, Belvedere ..... (10's & over par) ½
[J. Kinney, Pres., J. Stuart, Cash.]
10's, altered from 2's Hold them up to the light.
20's, a Proof sheet of the genuine plate with counterfeit signatures; paper poor.

Burlington County Bank, Medford .... do
[Benj. Shreve, Pres., J. Oliphant, Cash.]
There are frauds which read "real estate pledged & private property holden" between the officers names.
5s, vig. eagle on a rock surrounded by water—paper poor. These read "Burlington Co. Bank,"—in the genuine the County is written out in full.
5s, vig. a female, emblem of Hope. This is spurious.
10s, vig. an Indian viewing a locomotive and cars. These read "Burlington Co. Bank,"—in the genuine the County is written out in full.

Commercial Bank, Perth Amboy, ... (10's par) do
[Herman Bruen, Pres., J. A. Nichols, Cash.]
☞ Bills of ALL denominations on this bank, altered from broken Commercial Bank, Millington, Md.
3's, let. A. pay to bearer. Perth Amboy is printed in two places in the centre of the bill.
3's, let. A. pay to John Bruen. May 12, 1823; others, July, 1823 pay S. Dam Whitehead, Cash.
3's, pay to H. Burr, Nov. 4, 1823; others, pay to W. Edgar, Jan. 20, 1827.
3's, lett. A. The waves aside of the ship are rough and dotted. One of the trees stands inclined, and the top touches the oval on the right of the note.
5s, vig Neptune in his car drawn by sea-horses.
3's, lett. D. pay J. Marsh or bearer, March 1, 1831, Wm. Whitehead, Cash., J. Parker, President.
5's, pay to Wm. Edgar, Jan. 20, 1827.
5's, letter A. pay to J. Marsh, dated March 1, 1831, signed Wm. Whitehead, Cash., J. Parker, Pres.
10's, altered from 1's—vig. 4 ships and a steamboat, city in the distance.

Cumberland Bank of N. J., Bridgetown, ... do
[J. B. Potter, Pres., W. G. Nixon, Cash.]
1's, letts. E. e. dated Jan. 8, 1840; paper dark, marginal engraving poor.
1's, letts. F. f. various dates. The bottom of the "J" in JERSEY; just below the "E"—"PROMISS" is ⅓ of an inch from the left margin, in the genuine it almost touches it.
3's, let. G. Jan. 8, 1840, signatures poor. Attached to the L in "Cumberland," is but one flourish; in the genuine there are two flourishes.
3's, paper inferior, and the whole appearance bad.
5's, lett. A. pay H. Knox, No. 3940, dated Bridgetown, March 1, 1817, C. Read. Cash. James Giles. Pres.
5s, altered from Comm. Bk, Millington; vig. reapers, &c.

Delaware Bridge Co., Lambertville... broke 70
[A. St. Johns. Pres., S. M. Robinson, Cash.]
☞ Failed Dec. 27, 1847, at 10 o'clock, a. m.

Farmers' Bank of N. Jer., Mount Holly ..... ½
[John Black, Pres., J. Beatty, Cash.]
☞ Bills of the broken Farmers of Seneca County, altered to this bank, "Mount Holly" stamped on.
5's, vig. arms of the State—the vig. of the genuine has cattle and sheep.
5's & 10's, spurious. Vignette, a female. Durand & Co., engravers—altered from Farmers' Bank Seneca co. N. Y., a broken bank.
10's, altered from 1's. Have the heads of Washington and Franklin. The vignette of the true 10's is a distant view of a ship, a church, and several buildings.

Farm. & Mech. Bar alhway, ... (10's par) do
[J. O. Lufbery, Pres., B ...., Cash.]
5's, altered; vig. female with a child.
5's, altered; F. King, pres., Wm. Edgar, cash.—the genuine are engrav'd by Rawdon, Wright & Co. N. Y.
20's, altered; vig. a black smith—officers' names are counterfeited and there is a dog's head between them. The genuine are light.

Far. & Mer., Middletown Point, ... (5's & over, par) ¼
[Asbury Fountain, Pres., Elihu Baker, Cash.]
3's, vig. a female, shenf ... wheat, axe, screw, &c. Washington on one end, and a lady on the other.
5's, vig. a female sitting. bales of goods, shipping, &c. Washington and Lafayette on the ends.

N. Jersey

NEW-JERSEY.

Farm. & Mech. Bank, New Brunswick,........ broke
Franklin Bank, Jersey City,.................worthless
Hoboken Bk'g & Grazing Co.,...........worthless
Jersey City Bank,..........................worthless
   Do.   pay at Ontario,...........worthless
Manufacturers' Bank, Belleville,............. broke

Mech. Bank of Burlington, Burlington,.... ½
[Wm. R. Allen, Pres., Geo. Gaskill, Cash.]
5's, let. A—of a pale, whitish cast, very indistinct engraving orlithograph; a sheep between the names of the officers—this is unlike the genuine in every particular.
5's, altered. vig. rail cars, &c., with the lion and unicorn.
10's, vig. Neptune & lady in a car drawn by sea-horses.
10's, vig. two human figures, a winged animal on a chest.
20's, vig. a figure of a female sitting at a spinning wheel; Indian on the right margin, female and eagle on the left. Engraved by Burton & Gurley, N. York.

Mechanics' Bank, Newark,......(5's & over, par) do
[Joseph A. Halsey, Pres., M.W. Day, Cash.]
3s. good imitation of genuine; officers' names engraved, but the cashier's is retraced with a pen; very likely to pass.
5's, lett. B. altered from the Mechanical Bank of St. Johns, L. C. G. Hosmer, Cash., H. N. Warren, Pres.
10's, let. B. vig. a blacksmith, &c., a dog below—Toppan Carpenter & Co., is spelt Topham, Carpenter & Co.
10's, altered from 2's—vig. a woman sitting in the field holding a child—reapers in the distance.
10's, let. A. Mathias W. Day, cash., J. A. Halsey, pres. rail car on left & steam ship on right end—poorly done.
50's, lett. B. altered from 1's, pay Wm. Wright.

Mechanics' Bank, Paterson,...............worthless

Mech. & Manuf. Bk, Trenton,....(5s & over par) ½
[George Hill, Pres., T. Abbott, Cash.]
5's, let. B., vig. arms of the state, and rail cars.
10's, altered from ones. The ones have for a vig. a horse, and on both ends a drove of sheep.

Monmouth Bank, Freehold,................ fraud

Morris Canal & Banking Co.,............. fraud

Morris Conn. Bank, Morristown,.....(10's par) do
[H. A. Ford, Pres., T. T. Wood, Cash.]
3's, altered from 1s—Oct. 1, 1843—Thos. F. Wood, cash.; Henry A. Ford, pres.—No. 148.
2's, v. g. female reclining on sheaves of wheat—Burton & Gurley, N. Y., engravers.
5's, altered from 1s—the "S" on "dollars," is not in proportion, and "five" is bad.
10's, altered—vig. a female riding in a car.
10's, altered from 1's. Detected by the "S" after the word dollars, which is badly done.
20's, altered from 1's; vig. a goddess holding a staff; "twenty dollars," and the figures "20," are defective.

Newark Bank & Ins. Co.....(5's & over, par) do
[John Taylor, Pres., J. D. Vermilye, Cash.]
2's, lett. C. pay D. Nichols, Jan. 9, 1822. Look out for these, as the letter has been altered to G.
2's, lett. C. pay to S. Nichols. Jan. 9, 1822.
2's, lett. C. pay to S. Grant, Feb. 4, 1826.
2's, lett. D. pay to J. Sanford, Jan. 4, 1826.
2's, lett. D. pay to D. Nichols, July 3, 1826.
3's, lett. K. Jan. 9, 1822, pay to J. Sanford.
5's, altered from 1's, Oct. 21, 1834—hold to the light.
5's, altered from twos—easily detected.
10's, lett. O. altered from 1's, Oct. 21, 1334.
10's, lett. F. dated July 4, 1836.
10's, altered from 1's of the new emission.
20's, altered from 3's.

N. J. Manuf. & Bkg. Co., Hoboken,......worthless
N. J. Protection & Lombard B'k,......worthless
Orange Bank, Orange,........(5's & over, par) ½
[S. D. Day, Pres. Chas. G. Rockwood, Cash.]
3's, Louis M. Wiss. (others, Viss,) Cashi-r, W. A. Thompson, Pres. Alter'd from State Bank, Trenton.
5's, two figures, one sitting; eng. by N. Eng. Co.
5's, vig. shipping, warehouses, &c.—on the left an Indian and dog—engraved by Durand & Co.
10's, vig. stores, shipping, &c., a female on the left end; engraved by Durand & Co.

People's Bank, Paterson,.................... ?
[E. B. D. Ogden, Pres., H. C. Stimson, Cash.]
3's, altered from 1's—vig. a family group in harvest; the genuine have a man ploughing.
3's, altered from 1s, new plate; has Washington in a square frame on the left; genuine 5 has not got him.
5's, lett. A. May 12, 1830, pay T. S. Avery. Others March 12 1839. Paper thin, dull appearance.
10's, lett. B. altered from 2's.

Plainfield Bank, Plainfield............(closed.) 60
[Nathan Vail, Pres. Henry D. Beach, Cash.]
17 The time for selling or presenting these notes will expire on the 6th of February, 1848.

Princeton Bank, Princeton,................... ½
[R. S. Field, Pres., L. P. Smith, Cash.]
5's, count., Louis P. Smith, Cash., R. S Field, Pres. "Five dollars" in large capitals on them.
10's, altered from Globe Bank, New-York; a careful examination will easily detect them.

Salem Banking Company, Salem,......... do
[Calvin Belden, Pres., Geo. C. Rumsay, Cash.]
1's, lett. A. pay G. Scull, July 1, 1840. Well done.
1's, lett. B. pay to E. Ware, dated Jan. 1, 1830, Jno. Elwell, Cash., Calvin Belden, Pres. Paper thick with a yellow shade. Engraving bad.
5's, lett. A. pay T. Jones, April 6, 1838, John Elwell, Cash., Calvin Belden. Pres. Vignettes dim and coarse.
5's, lett. B. pay to S. Brown, dated Oct. 1, 1839.
5's, altered from 1's. The vignette of the genuine 5's is the coat of Arms of the States.
10's, altered from 1's. Vignette, an ox; on the true 10's is the Arms of the State.

Salem & Phil. Manuf. Co., Salem,.........worthless
State Bank, Camden,.......................... ½
[John Gill, Pres., Auley M'Calla, Cash.]
1's, wood cut. Dark impression.
5's, lett. D. pay to J. Adams, Jan. 7, 1822
10's, lett. H. pay to Jonas Smith, Jan. 3, 1814.
10's, lett. C. pay to J. Cam, May 1, 1830.
10's, lett. B. pay to I. Kane, May 1, 1830.
20's, let. C. dated Jan. 1, 1828, altered from 1's. The word TWENTY is in German text, and the letter "S" in the words "Dollars," is clumsily done.

State Bank, Elizabethtown,......(5's & over, par) do
[Charles Davis, Pres., James Crane, Cash.]
1's, lett. C. Sept. 4, 1837, pay J. Reed—James Crane, Cash. Some pay P. Smith, May 3, 1826; they appear to be a new emission of the old plate. They are badly filled up. Also, some pay to R. Lee, May 4, 1823.
10's, altered from 1's—"TEN DOLLARS" is defective —general appearance good, & well calculated to pass.

State B'k at Morris, Morristown,.....(10's par) do
[W. N. Wood, Pres., W. A. Carmichael, Cash.]
1's, lett. B. pay to J. J. Scofield, Feb. 1, 1838—E. Condit, Cash., Silas Condit, Pres.
2's, lett. D. pay to S. Southard, July 1, 1823.
3's, lett. F. to whom pay unknown, Oct. 1, 1823.
3's, lett. D. pay to Jos. Cutler, May 1, 1824.
5's, figures and paper bad. The 5's enclosed in the lower medallions are both leaning.
10's, lett. H. June 2, 1812; "AT MORRIS" is written with a pen. Some filled up to State B'k at Trenton, April 1, 1813.
10's alt'd from 1's, the repetition of "ONE" on top & bottom margins, is cut off—the S in Dollars is crowded.

State Bank, Newark,............(5's & over, par) do
[E. Van Arsdale, Pres., Wm. H. Mott, Cash.]
1's, let. D. pay at the Mechanics' Bank, New-York, Sep. 1, 1838, A. G. Halsey, cash., Elias Van Arsdale, pres., payable to Jno. Fleming, engraved—vig. a stone cutter at work.
5's, lett. F. pay at Mechanics' Bank, New-York.
5's, vignette, an Indian sitting, engraved by Jones, N.Y. The genuine were engraved in Philadelphia.
5's, lett. I. Nov. 15, 1831, pay to W. Wright.
1 i's, altered from ones. Well done.
10's, lett. A., Vermilye, cash., Van Arsdale, pres. Under President's name are the words "Jones, Co N.Y."—paper thin, and general appearance bad.

State Bank, New-Brunswick,......(5's & over, par) do
[F. R. Smith, Pres., John B. Hill, Cash.]
2's, vig. the coat of arms of the state of New Jersey.
5's, lett. D. dated Oct. 1, 1830, Sep. 12, 1815; others 1819.
5's, lett. E. D. pay S. Bishop; some let. E. Feb. 12, 1821.
10's, lett. A. pay J. Marsh, altered from 1's.
10's, letter B. pay to P. V. Pool, dated January 25, 1818. Others, pay to I. Bishop, dated Feb. 1, 1822.
10's, letter B. Others letter F. filled up to various persons and dates.

State Bank, Trenton,.......................worthless

Sussex Bank, Newtown,........(10's & over, par) ½
[David Ryerson, Pres., S. D. Morford, Cash.]
1s, vig. a man, oxen, plough, &c., Burton & Gurley, eng'rs.
1's, lett. B. pay D. Ford, dated March 1, 1822.
5's, lett. B. pay Corn's. Smith or b'arer, Aug. 30, 1830.
5's, lett. D. dated May 21, 1830, pay C. Smith.
5's, lett. D. pay to Cor's Smith, May 4, 1831.
10s, poor imitation, vig. an Indian surprised at a locomotive and cars; a ship on the right end, and an Indian with a bow on the left—let. A—Rawdon, Wright & Hatch, as engravers.

Trenton Bk'g Co. Trenton,......(5's & over, par) do
[Phil. Dickinson, Pres., T. J. Stryker, Cash.]
1s, an alteration; vig. a man ploughing with oxen; the words UNE PIASTRE, are repeated at the top of the note
1's, vig. a man ploughing, oxen and trees in the distance, with a female on one end and an Indian on the other.
2's, let. B. vig. a dog over a dead deer—entirely different from the genuine.
5's, let. A. vig. an eagle on a rock, on the right a vessel on the left a locomotive. A sleeping dog is at the bottom, with "Trenton" over him. The genuine have "Trenton Banking Comp'y" and no dog.
10s, vig. a man in a sitting posture, and a ship—English coat of arms between the signatures.

5's, let. B. various dates, and pay to different persons—genuine have a streak of red, the spurions have not.
5's and **10's**, altered from broken Canada bank notes, having the lion and unicorn; forged signatures; engraved by Harris & Sealy, N. Y.
10's, vig. Indian and rail cars, ship on the right.

Union Bank, Dover,.......................... ½
[G. M. Hinchman, Pres., T. B. Segur, Cash.]
2s, vig. an inclined plane, acqueduct on the right.
3's, altered from ones—the vignette of the true three is an oval filled with dairy maids.
5's, let. A—the female's face in the vignette is poorly executed—date is spelt JULI, 1839 the two last figures blotted.
5's, lett. A. pay to H. Brucon; figure 5 at the top of the bill is larger than genuine.
10's, altered from Globe Bank, N. Y.; Durand & Co. at the bottom of the note.
Washington Bkg. Co., Hackensack,........worthless

PENNSYLVANIA.

Relief Notes, (4th of May act,)................... 3

Agricultural Bank, Great Bend,...........worthless

Allegany Bank of Penn., Bedford,........worthless

Bank of Beaver,.........................worthless

Bank of Chambersburgh,.................. 2
[T. G. McCulloh, Pres., James Lesly, Cash]
5s, it reads 'Chambersburgh Bank,' &c. instead of 'The Bank of Chambersburgh.'—vig. a female and child.
Bank of Commerce, Philadelphia,............. ½
[Geo. Follen, Pres., J. C. Donnell, Cash.]
5s, vig. an eagle; nothing like the genuine
5s, altered, vig. two females, with key & safe; "real estate pledged & private property holden," betw'n signatures
10's, let. A. train of cars on the left, agricultural implements on the right; "10" on the four corners, and "secured by real estate and mortgage," etc. in a circle at the bottom.
Bank of Chester County, Westchester,...... ½
[Wm. Darlington, Pres., D Townsend, Cash.]
10's, let. A. lithograph, vig. female with wings, paper of a red cast—"Westchester" blurred—has Rawdon, Wright & Hatch, as engravers, who never worked for this bank.
10's, altered, vig. Declaration of Independence.
20's, altered, vignette a blacksmith at his forge.
Bank of Delaware County, Chester,........ ½
[Jesse J. Maris, Pres., F. J. Hinkson, Cash.]
20's, altered from 5's. Calculated to deceive.
50's, altered from 5's, pay T. Clyde, Jan. 1, 1836.
Bank of Germantown,...................... do
[Saml. Harvey, Pres. J. F. Watson, Cash.]
20's, altered from 5's. Hold them to the light.
Bank of Gettysburg, Gettysburg,............ 1¼
[Robert Smith, Pres., J. B. M'Pherson, Cash.]
5's, let. I. pay R. Smith, Nov. 14, 1828, some 1829. Paper lighter, thinner, & softer than the genuine, without the circular water mark therein.
Bank of Lewistown,.........................
[John Potter, Pres., R. F. Ellis, Cash.]
Bank of Middletown, Middletown,........... 1½
[Mercer Brown, Pres., Simon Cameron, Cash.]
5's, engraving coarse. In the first batch the "M" in "Middletown" on the upper left margin, had an EXTRA flourish, which has since been taken off, to make it correspond with the genuine—this leaves the "M" an ¼ of an inch further from the margin than in the true bill, in which it is close on to it
5's, an alteration; vig. a female with a child.
10's, altered vig. signing declaration of independence
20's, alteration; vig. blacksmith, &c.
Bank of Montgomery County, Norristown,.. ½
[J. Boyer, Pres., W. H. Slingluff, Cash.]
5's, let. B. vig. railroad, &c.; an Indian on the left, Liberty on the right. The general appearance poor.
5's, letter A. pay to J. Wells, Nov. 1, 1823. Others, 1825. Others, in 1826. Some, May 2, 1826.
5's, lett. B. pay to W. Webb, dated July 2, 1825.
10's, let. A vig. a female, spinning wheel, &c., "Pennsylvania" and "Norristown" defective.
Bank of North America, Philadelphia,....... do
[J. Richardson, Pres., J. Hockley, Cash.]
5's, let. H. pay T. Folwell, vig. Justice and Liberty. On each end a female holding a scroll, &c.
10's, letts. A. I. pay to J. Oat, March 2, 1827.
10's, lett. A. pay to J. Mann, March 26, 1827.
Bank of Northern Liberties, Phil'a.,........ do
[R. L. Pitfield, Pres., S. W. Caldwell, Cash.]
5's, altered. Signed F. Roberts, cash.
10's, alt'd from 1's. let. B—examine the figures "10," and "payable on demand"—both altered.
10's, spurious—they read "Northern Liberties Bank," the genuine read "Bank of Northern Liberties."
10's, let. A. pay S. Starr, July 4, 1838; pale ink of a yellow tinge. R. L. Pitfield, Ch., J. Knight, Pr. Poorly engrv'd.
10's. let. C. pay J. Taylor, Oct. 18, 1837 R. L. Pitfield, cash., J. Knight, pres—left end, Neptune in a car; on right a wagoner—Cash.'s signature is stiff; President's is too large.

Bank of Northumberland,................... ½
[John Taggart, Pres., J. R. Priestly, Cash.]
5's, alte'd from a broken concern; vig. a female holding a child; "Northumberland" defective.
5's, altered from 1's, relief note, vignette, a female holding a goblet to an eagle.
10's, vig. declaration of independence; on the right end a blacksmith & forge; on the left a sailor with a flag.
20's, vig. Pat Lyon & forge, cars in distance; right end cattle; left, railroad cars.

Bank of Pennsylvania, Philadelphia,........ do
[Jos. Trotter, Pres., Geo. Philler, Cash.]
5s, vig. a female sitting on boxes, and a ship under sail; Washington and Lafayette on the ends.
5's, altered from 10th Ward Bank, N. Y.; J. Froth, pres. "Bank of Pennsylvania" defective—vig. female and child.
5's, lett. F. 8, J. Trotter. Cash., Josh. Norris, Pres. Paper poor, impression light. engraving coarse.
5's, lett. M. pay to G. W. Warder, April 2, 1836.
10's, altered, vig. signing declaration of independence.
10's, letter F. pay to S. Bray, J. Frith, Cash., Jos. A. Norris, Pres., dated Aug. 16, 1836.
10's, lett. C. pay to H. Clay, April 16, 1836.
10, let. E. pay to the order of H. Clay—April 16, 1833, J. Trotter, cash., Joseph Norris. pres.
10.s, letter A. April 8th, 1833, pay H. Mar. In the word President the letter E is larger than the rest,
10's, let. B. April 23, 1833—likeness of Franklin imperfect & the letters in the words Independence & Liberty also.
20's, altered from 10th Ward Bank—engraving good.
50's, lett. C. pay to J. Boone, March 22, 1812.

Bank of Penn Township, Philadelphia,...... do
[E. Dallett, Pres., J. Russell, Cash.]
10's, Washington on the LEFT—is on the right in genuine.
20's, well done. Franklin's likeness on right margin, is coarsely engraved, various dates.

Bank of Pittsburgh, Pittsburgh,.............. 2
[J. Graham, Pres., J. Snyder, Cash.]
5's, lett. C. pay to H. Baldwin, May 4, 1835.
5's, lett. C. March 3, 1827—vig. a blacksmith, anvil, &c.
5's, let. C. pay to S. H. Scott, original date altered with a pen to 1828, John M'Donald, Pres.
10's, lett. C. pay to M. Andrews, Oct. 17 1815.
20's, vig. a female leaning on an urn filled with flowers.

Bank of Swatara, Harrisburgh,.............worthless

Bank of the U. S., Phil............(winding up) 30
[J. Robertson, Pres, T. S. Taylor, Cash.]
☞ Most of the bills of this Bank having been redeemed we have withdrawn the descriptions of counterfeits. Persons unacquainted with the bills had better refuse them.

Bank of Washington,......................worthless
Berk's County Bank, Reading,..............worthless

Carlisle Bank, Carlisle,........................ 1½
[Geo. A. Lyon, Pres., W. S. Cobean, Cash.]
Centre Bank of Penn., Bedford,............worthless
City Bank, Pittsburgh,........................worthless
Columbia Bk. & Bridge Co., Columbia,..... ½
[John N. Lane, Pres., Samuel Shock, Cash.]
10s. good imitation of genuine; Lafayette on the right, steamboat and two children on the left—appears blurred.
100's, alte'd from 5's, vig. Mercury & a female, bales of goods, ship, &c.—genuine have a large female figure.

Columbia Bank, Milton,.........................worthless

Commercial Bank of Pa., Philadelphia,.... ½
[James Dundas, Pres., J. J. Cope, Cash.]
☞ Bills of ALL denominations, on this bank, altered from broken Comm. Bank, Millington, Md.
10's, **20's** & **50's**, alte'd from 5's; none but the 5's have for a vignette Penn's Treaty with the Indians.
10's, lett. C. pay to H. Clay, dated Jan. 8, 1824.
10's, old plate—the 10's now issued have miniatures of Washington and Franklin for a vignette.
10's, let. A. pay Geo. W. Ash, March 2, others, June 2, 1830.
20's, well done, Smith Cash , paper whiter than genuine.
50's, altered from 5's, dated June 8, 1832.

Doylestown Bank, Doylestown,................ do
[E. Dubois, Pres., D. Byrnes, Cash.]
5's, altered, vig a female and child; engraving good.
5's, altered, B. Byrns, cash., W. Williams, pres.
10's, altered, vig. declaration of independence.
20's, letter A—vig. blacksmith and forge—on the right end cattle, &c. on the left railroad and train. The title of the bank light impression and blotted.
50's, vig. female, shipping, steamboat, &c. W. E. Tucker & Co. engravers—they never engraved for this bank.

Easton Bank, Easton,.......................... par
[Thos. M'Keen. Pres., J. Sinton, Cash.]
5's, lett. C. dated Aug. 1, 1827, pay to O. Rice.
10's, lett. C. pay to J. Post dated Feb. 1, 1824.
Erie Bank, Eric,.................................. 3
[G. McSparren, Cash.]
5's, relief notes, altered from 1's and 2's.
10's, let. A. vig. Perry's victory; engraving coarse. Not like any of the genuine.

Exchange Bank, Pittsburgh,.................... 1½
[Wm. Robinson, Jr., Pres., T. M. Howe, Cash.]
2's. relief notes—has but one bold shade on "2" on left margin—genuine has a slight second shade on said figure.
5's, lett. B., vig. figure of justice with scales—May 9, 1843, the president, Robinson, badly done.
5's, Spurious, W. Robing, pres., J. Foster, cash.

Exch. Bank, Branch, Hollidaysburgh,........ 2
[John Foster, Pres., Wm. Williams, Cash.]
5's, let. A. vig. a sailor leaning against an anchor; the genuine notes have two females.
5's, lett. B. pay, some to R. Nash; others, to R. Lansing; and others, to Wm. B. Wallis, dated June 1, 1836, J. Forster, Cash., W. Robinson, Pres.
10's, vignette, Perry's victory.

Exch. Bank & Savings Ins., Phila.,......worthless

Farmers' Bank of Bucks Co. Bristol,...... ½
[J. Paxson, Pres., R. C. Beatty, Cash.]
5's, dated at Bristol, instead of Hulmeville, March 1, 1828.
10's, let. B. pay different persons, & various dates.

Farm. Bank of Lancaster, Lancaster,....... ½
[G. H. Krug, Pres., Gerardus Clarkson, Cash.]
5's, lett. A. dated March 7, 1832, pay to J. Wind. Others, March 17, 1831, pay to Geo. H. King.
10's & **50**'s, alt'd from 5's of the above counterfeit.

Farmers' Bank of Reading,................ do
[Isaac Eckert, Pres., H. H. Muhlenberg, Cash.]
5's, let. A. pay G. Ludwig, Jan. 1, 1835, Geo. McKeen, Ch. Beuverille Kein. Pr.—paper has silk mark; fair appearance.
5's, let. D. pay G. Smith, Jan. 1, 1833; engraving coarse.
100's, lett. A. pay to John Hanold or bearer.

Farmers' Bank of Schuylkill County,.... do
[Geo. Rahn, Pres., Jos. W. Cake, Cash.]

Farmers' & Drov. B., Waynesburgh.......... 3
[A. Buchanan, Pres., J. Lazear, Cash.]

Farmers' & Mech. Bank, Philadelphia,...... ½
[Joseph Tagert, Pres., Wm. Patton, Jr. Cash.]
5's, let. A. vig. female, cows, farm-house, &c. Likely to pass.
5's, alte'd from Farmers' & Mechanics' Bank, Wisconsin.
20's, altered, vig. a female spinning; on the left a female holds a cup to an eagle Engraved by Burton & Gurley.
20's, lett. A. dated Nov. 20, 1834, pay G. Hurl.
20's, letter E. No. 89, Nov. 29, 1834. They are on red paper; execution of the engraving bad.
50's, altered—"State of Pennsylvania" and "Philadelphia," are evidently stamped on.

Farm. & Mech. Bank, N. Salem,............worthless
Farm. & Mech. Savings Ins., Phila.,......worthless
Farm. & Mech. Bank, Greencastle,........worthless
Farm. & Mech. Bank, Pittsburgh,..........worthless
Franklin Savings Bank, Philadel.,........worthless

Franklin Bank, Washington,.................. 2
[T. M. T. McKennan, Pres., J. Marshel, Cash.]
5's, lett. A. pay to R. Wylie, dated Nov. 1, 1836.

Girard Bank, Philadelphia,.................. ½
50's, altered from 5's. Hold them to the light.

Girard Loan Co., Philadelphia,.............worthless

Harrisburgh Bank, Harrisburgh,........... 1½
[Thomas Elder, Pres., J. W. Weir, Cash.]
10's, lett. A. May 4, 1829, pay J. E. Whiteside.
10's vignette a steamboat, rail road cars, &c.
20's, let. A, pay J. W. Wier, Feb. 7, 1839. In the genuine, the third Twenty on lower margin commences immediately under "r" in cash'r—in bad one under "h."

Harmony Institute,..........................worthless

Honesdale Bank, Honesdale,.................. 1
[R. L. Seeley, Pres., S. D. Ward, Cash.]
5's, altered; vig. a female holding a child.
10's, altered; "X," "10" & a locomotive on the left end; On the genuine the letters TEN are across the left end.
10's, altered; vig. siguing Declaration of Independece; the genuine has Vulcan with his sledge.
20's, an alterion vig. a blacksmith and sledge. All genuine notes are engraved by Rawdon, Wright & Hatch.

Huntington Bank,..........................worthless

Juniata Bank of Penn., Lewistown,......worthless

Kensington Bank, Philadelphia,.............. ½
[J. Wainwright, Pres., C. Keen, Cash.]
5's, vig. two figures; on the right a female with a staff, on the left a female with a rake, jug, &c.
5's, altered—have "real estate pledged & private property holden" between the signatures; not on the genuine.
5's, vig. reapers in a field—female with sickle, on the ends.
5's, vig. three females, representing Agriculture, &c.—engraved by Terry, Pelton & Co.
10's, vig Neptune on his car; Industry and Prosperity on the right end, rail cars, &c. on the left.
10's, vig spread eagle—Terry, Pelton & Co. engravers.
10's, vig. railcars, &c. J. Wood, Pr., Stacy A Paxon, Ch.

Lancaster Bank, Lancaster,.................... ½
[David Longenecker, Pres., Christ. Bachman, Cash.]
☞ Frauds altered from a Canada concern, engraved by Harris & Sealy. Vignette, a lion and unicorn.
5s, vig. three females, Lafayette & Franklin on the ends.
5's, vig. shipping, &c.—the genuine is different.
5's, altered, vig. female & child. Counterfeit signatures.
5's & **10**'s, altered, vig. the lion and unicorn
10's, altered—vig. shipping, warehouses, &c.
10's, vig. a spread eagle—the genuine is different.
50's, lett. A., altered from 5's, Oct. 3, 1836.
50's, altered from the Southwark Savings Institution. F. Roberts, Cash., G. F. Benckhert, Pr.

Lancaster County, Bank, Lancaster,........ do
[John Landes, Pres., R. D. Carson, Cash.]
5's, **10**'s, **20**'s, & **50**'s, altered from Southwark Savings Ins.; genuine have Robt. D. Carson, cash. J. Landes, pres.

Lancaster Loan Co.,.......................worthless

Lebanon Bank, Lebanon,....................... ½
[J. W. Gloninger, Pres., George Gleim, Cash.]
5's, altered from the broken Gallipolis (O.) Bank. Engraved by Rawdon, Wright & Hatch.
5's, vig. female with a child.
10's, vig. the declaration of independence—blacksmith on the right, sailor with a flag on the left.
20's, vig. railroad cars, blacksmith and forge.

Lehigh County Bank, Allentown,....(closed) —
[M. Y. Beach, Pres., A. Beach, Cash.]

Lumberman's Bank, Warren...............worthless

Manuf. & Mech. Bank, Philadelphia,...... ½
[John Farr, Pres., M. W. Woodward, Cash.]
5's, letter A., No. 470.
5's, vig. a female, boxes, and a vessel under sail. Heads of Washington & Lafayette on the ends.
10's, altered from 5s. Hold them to the light.
50's, alt'd from 5's—FIFTY is crooked, & badly put on.
50's, let. A, pay H. Wilson, Jan. 5, 1846; the signatures of the officers are poor imitations of the genuine.

Manual Labor Bank. Philadelphia,........worthless
Marietta & Susquch. Trading Co.,......worthless

Mech. Bank of City of Philadelphia,..... ½
[J. B. Mitchell, Pres., William Thaw, Cash.]
3's, let. A.—the "THREE" on the right end is defective.
5's, the spurious read "Mechanics' Bank," omitting "the city and county of Philadelphia."
10's, altered, vig. a train of cars. Others, with an eagle.
20's, altered from a broken bank, and read "Mechanics Bank will pay," &c., omitting "city of Philadelphia."
20's, lett. C. Oct. 3, 1828, pay Wm. Lee—Henry Clay on the left border, and Washington on the right
50's, let. C. altered from 5's. Observe, "FIFTY" is put too close to the letter D in Dollars.
100's, vig. three females joining hands—right end a female and eagle; left, an eagle and shield—genuine have the heads of Penn on the right, and Morris on the left.

Merchants' & Manuf. Bank, Pittsburgh..... 1½
[Thomas Scott, Pres., W. H. Denny, Cash.]
5s, let. A, imitation of genuine—female in centre & on the right end, a man with a hammer on the left—various dates.

Merchants' Bank, Philadelphia,............worthless

Miners' Bank of Pottsville,................ ½
[J. Shippen, Pres., Charles Loeser, Cash.]
5's, let. F., variously filled up.
5's, altered from the Hazleton Coal Company, signed R. Miner, Treas., Samuel Moore, Pres.
5's, Aug. 1, 1840, pay J. White. Paper thin, reddish appearance. Engraving good. Signatures bad.
50's, medallion head on left end—vig. of genuine is a female, with "50" worked in, and two females on each side.

Monongahela Bank, Brownsville,............ 2
[J. L. Bowman, Pres., D. S. Knox, Cash.]
2's, Relief notes, well executed—paper bluish.
50's. The bank has no $50 notes out.

Moyamensing Bank, Philadelphia....(closing) ½
20's, altered; vig. a blacksmith and anvil.

New Salem Bank, Fayette Co.,............worthless

Northampton Bank,.......................worthless
Northern Bank. Penn., Dundaff,..........worthless
Northumberland Union,..................worthless
N. W. Bank of Pennsylvania,............worthless
Pennsylvania Savings Bank,............worthless
Penn. Agricultural & Manuf. Bank,....worthless

Philadelphia Bank,........................ ½
[Samuel F. Smith, Pres., John B. Trevor, Cash.]
5's, lett. C. pay to T. Wurtz, dated Feb. 9, 1824.
5's, lett. C. pay to S. Tice, dated June 4, 1824.
10's, letter C. pay J. James and R. Shade, Sept. 7, 1819, others Dec. 8, 1820, same officers.
10's, lett. D. dated Feb. 8, 1832, pay to D. Evans—D. Campbell, Cash. J. Reed, Pres.

10's, altered from 5's—vig. two females sitting down.
20's, altered from 5's.
20's, old plate, lett. E. pay to D. Edwin, May 9, 1814, 1824, 1825, and others in 1827.
500's, altered, vig. two females reaping, &c.—genuine is different. The names of the officers counterfeited.

Philadelphia Loan Co.,.................. worthless
Philadelphia Manufacturing Comp..... worthless
Philadelphia Savings Institution,...... worthless

Pittsburgh City Scrip,...................... 6

Pottsdam Manufacturing Co............ worthless
Richards' (Mark) **Checks**, Philadelphia,...... worthless

Schuylkill Bank, Philadolphia,................ ½
[J. Price Witherill, Pres.]
5's, lett. A. dated Sept. 1, 1830, signed J. H Levis, Cash., W. Meredith, Pres. Vignette coarse.
5's, lett. D. No. 1296, pay to Wm. Jones or bearer, dated Philadelphia, July 4, 1831.
20's, lett., to whom pay and date unknown.

Silver Lake Bank, Montrose,.............. worthless

Southwark Bank, Philadelphia,............... ½
[Thos. Sparks, Pres., Jas. S. Smith, Jr., Cash.]
5's, spurious, Roberts, Cash., Burkett, Pres.
10's, altered, F. Roberts, cash. F. Burkett, pres.

Southwark Savings Bank,.............. worthless

Susquehanna Co. Bank, Montrose,...... broke 40

Taylorsville Del. Bridge Co., Taylorsville,.. 25

Towanda Bank, Towanda,.................... fraud
Union Bank of Pennsylvania, Uniontown,. worthless

Western Bank, Philadelphia,............... ½
[J. Patterson, Pres., G. M. Troutman, Cash.]
5's, altered, vig. a female, bales of goods, and ship; Washington on left and Lafayette on the right end. The words "Western Bank,' are not on a straight line.
10's, let. A. No. 2406, June 10, 1843—it is the 16th of an nch wider and a little longer than the genuine—engraving coarse. Others, well done.
10's, vig. an eagle with extended wings, rail cars in the back ground—whole appearance bad.
10's, lett. D., Aug. 1, 1842, pay W. H. Steover. Joseph Patterson, Pres. A very good imitation.
20's, detected by the engravers—Terry, Pelton & Co.
500's, altered from a defunct concern.

West Branch Bank, Williamsport............. 3
[John C. Oliver, Pres., T. W. Lloyd, Cash.]
10's, let. D; vig. an eagle—paper whitish, filling up and president's name in fine band.

Westmoreland Bank, Greensburgh,........ worthless
Wilkesbarre Bridge Co.,..................... worthless

Wyoming Bank, Wilkesbarre,................. 2½
[G. Hollenbach, Pres., Edw. Lynch, Cash.]

York Bank, York,.............................. 1½
[James Lewis, Pres., Samuel Wagner Cash.]
☞ No **1**'s out, except some relief notes.
5s, let. B; old plate; dated Feb. 2, 1830, payable to W. Wagner, which is spelt Wagnor.

Youghogany Bank, Perryopolis............. worthless

DELAWARE.

☞ 1, 2, & 3 dollar notes of the Delaware Banks,.... 1

Bank of Delaware, Wilmington,............. ⅜
[H. Latimer, Pres., S. Floyd, Cash.]
1's, let. C. pay J. T. Baily, Nov. 2, 1839, U. Warner, Cash. Joseph Baily, Pres.—filling up & signatures lithographed.
2's, letter A. pay to W. S. Poole, dated July 7, 1839, signed Wm. Paxon, Cash., Jos. Baily, Pres.
2's, lett. C. The word "TO," immediately after "PAY ON DEMAND," has been left out.
2's, let. A. pay S. Floyd, Nov. 10, 1839, Warner, cash., Baily, pres. Lithographed, except the filling up and signatures.
2's, letter C. pay to J. T. Bailey, dated Sept. 9, 1839, signed H. Warner, Cash., Jos. Baily, Pres.
3's, vig. two men cradling; Washington on the right, Jupiter with a staff in his hand on the left.
3's, lett. D.—Sept. 9, 1837, the signatures of Wm. Paxson, cash., and Jos. Baily, pres., well executed.
5s, vig. a female and sailor, shippin in the distance Engraved by Terry, Pelton & Co.
5's, vig. a man in a sitting posture, naked from the neck to the loins, a cog-wheel on one side of him.
5's, altered from some broken concern; vig. an Indian and a man, separated by a shield—let. A.
5s, altered—vig. 3 females, with key, safe, &c.—between the signatures "real estate pledged and private property holden"
5's, vig. locomotive & cars; H. Latimer, Pr., S. Floyd, Ch.
5's, lett. D. pay to S. Knowles, Sept. 9, 1826.
10's, altered from a fraud; vig. "declaration of independence," which is not on the genuine.
10's, altered from 2's, vignette, a ship, a schooner and a steamboat; left end, head of Washington.
10's, let. Q, on the right; pay to W. Seal, Sept. 18, 1818. Well done.
10's, lett. A. Vignette three cows.
20's, let. A, vig. Indian & female—paper whitish & thin.
20s, altered from a fraud; vig. a blacksmith, &c.; on the left end locomotive and cars, with cattle, &c. on the right.
50's and **100**'s, altered from smaller notes.

Bank of Smyrna, Smyrna....................... ⅜
[Jacob Stout, Prest., A. Stockley, Cash.]
1's, let. D; March 7, 1844; T. Hook, cash. A. Smith, pres.
3's, vig. locomotive & cars; right end bull's head.
3's, lett. A. paper of a greasy cast—vig. a female with a sickle. In "to pay" the "t" is not crossed.
5's, let. C, vig. steam car, &c.—goddess of liberty on the right end. Appearance pale.
5's, altered from the 10th Ward Bank, N.Y.; the scratching may be seen on a close inspection.
5's, lett. A. vignette an eagle, engraving coarse.
10's, altered; vig. signing declaration of independence. "Smyrna," defective.
10's, let. A., vig. spread eagle, paper thin, engra. coarse.
20's, we have not seen them. It is said they can be detected by the word "The," before bank.

Farmers Bank of the State of Del., Dover, do
[H. M. Ridgely, Pres., James P. Wild, Cash.]
Branch at Georgetown, Isaac Tunnell, Cash.
Branch at Newcastle, H. J. Terry, Cash.
Branch at Wilmington, Robt. D. Hicks, Cash.

3's, let. E., pay —— Black, Dover, Mar. 4, 1823.
5's, lett. A. pay to Jos. Smithers, Jan. 19, 1825.
5's, lett. D. dated Wilming. pay to J. Ramsay.
20's altered from 3's—vig. a female representing Commerce; Justice on the right end.
50's, alt'd from 1's, vig. a female representing Commerce
50's altered from 10's. Easily detected, as the genuine bills are printed on red paper.

Laurel Bank,.................................. worthless

Union Bank of Delaware, Wilmington,.... ⅜
[E. W. Gilpin, Pres., W. P. Brobson, Cash.]
3's, altered from a red dog post note, Samuel Jones, pres't, James A. Bayard cash.
10's, altered from 1's. Vignette dairy maid surrounded with agricultural implements.
50's, altered from 1's—vig. a female, resting on a bucket; left end, a female and a figure one.

Wilmington & Brandywine Bank,...... do
[Geo. Bush, Pres., G. W. Sparks, Cash.]
1's, lett. B. pay M. Betts, dated March 30, 1840. The vignette is poorly engraved.
2's, letts. A. & B. variously filled up.
5's, lett. A., May, 1840, pay J. Jones.
5's, let. A. pay W. S. Hagany, Nov. 4, 1839, G. W. Sparks, cash. W. Seal, pres; right hand of the vig. landing of Columbus, is a small boat with a man in it; in the counterfeit it is scarcely perceptible.
5's, altered from ones—detected by the letter S. in the word "DOLLARS," which is badly done.
10s, has a steamboat, ship & sloop, with Webster's head.
10's altered from a broken bank plate; vig. an eagle and shield; left end, portrait of Washington.
20's, pay to C. Adams, some to J. Holt—lett. B—July 4, 1823, Evan Thomas, Cash. Jn. Torbert Pres.
20's, altered from 2's. Hold them to the light.

Wilmington Loan Co.,.................... worthless

MARYLAND.

Bank of Baltimore,............................ ½
[J. H. McCulloh, Pres., C. C. Jamison, Cash.]
5's, the letter O in BALTIMORE, on the right margin, is but half finished, and the E resembles a B.
10's, lett. B. variously dated and filled up.
10's, A. trebly lettered, pay to C. Kreel, Jan. 12, 1835. James Cox, cash., Wm. Lorman, pres.
10's, vig. Indian with a rifle. Others altered from 2s.
50's, let. B. altered from 5's, pay J. Carson, June 24, 1824. In the genuine 50's, "Bank of Baltimore," stands wholly in the SECOND line.
100's, lett. A., P. Littig, Cash., J. Bier, Pres.

Bank of Maryland, Baltimore,............... worthless

Bank of Salisbury, Salisbury,................ Broke

Bank of Westminster,........................ 2
[Isaac Shriver Pres., John Fisher, Cash.]
10's, OLD PLATE. Notice the letter N, in the numbering, in the genuine notes it is not perfect.

Caroline Bank, Denton,........................worthless

Chesapeake Bank, Baltimore,................ ½
[J. S. Gittings, Pres., J. Pinkney, Cash.]
3s, "Chesapeake," is spelt without the final E, and the ink on the name of the Bank and Baltimore, appears fresher than that on other parts of the note.
5s, altered, vig. a female holding a child.
5s, altered from the Commercial Bank of Millington.
10s, altered, vig. signing the declaration of independence.
10s, altered from smaller genuine notes.
20s, vig. a female, iron chest, &c. Purports to be engraved by Draper, Toppan & Co.

City Bank of Baltimore,..................worthless

Citizens' Bank, Baltimore,...................... ½
[William Reynolds, Pres., F. J. Dallam, Cash.]
2's, an alteration; Langdon, Cash., Johnson, Pres.
3's, spurious. The bank never issued any threes.

Cohen (J. I., jr. & Brothers.) **Bank**, Baltimore,...worthless
Commercial Bank of Baltimore,......worthless
Commercial Bank of Millington,......worthless

Com. & Far. Bank of Baltimore,.......... ½
[Elie Clagett, Pres., Trueman Cross, Cash.]
10's, let. B. Dec. 4, 1830; some Mar. 4, 1831. pay T. Cross
10's, good lithograph; vig. oxen and plough.

Conocheague Bank, Williamsport,........worthless

Cumberland Bank, Cumberland,.............. 2
[David Shriver, Pres., J. Shriver, Cash.]
5's, the spurious read "Cumberland Bank," the genuine adds "of Alleghany," in the same line.

Elkton Bank of Maryland,..............worthless

Farmers' Bank of Maryland, Annapolis,.. 1½
[Geo. Wells, Pres., T. Franklin, Cash.]
Branch at Easton, Wm. B. Smith, Cash.
Branch at Frederick, Cyrus Mantz, Cash.
1's, genuine has a "bee lit on a log"—counterfeit has no bee on the log. The bank should issue a new plate.
5's, let. B; vig. a female and sheaf of grain.
5's, lett. H. of Branch at Elkton, Sept. 4, 1834.
5's, letter D. of Branch at Easton, pay N. Hammond, April 27, 1827; others, Sept. 7, 1827.
10's, pay to J. C. Weems, dated Oct. 9, 1826.
10's, lett. B. dated at Fredericksburgh, Dec. 27, 1824, pay to J. Ryler, Joseph Pinkney, Cash.
20's, old plate, pay Thos. J. Bullett, Annapolis, April 8, 1839, Maynard, Cash., Harwood Pres.

Farmers' & Mech. Bank, Frederick,...... do
[William Tyler, Pres., Thos. W. Morgan, Cash.]
10's, vig. a man shoeing a horse. Spurious.
10s, vig. a man with a wheel, square, &c.; left end reapers.
100's, vig. a female and eagle; Washington on the left—Lafayette on the right. Burton & Gurley, engravers.

Farm. & Millers' Bank, Hagerstown,........Broke

Farmers' & Merch. Bank, Baltimore, ... ½
[J. H. Thomas, Pres., J. Loney, Cash.]
5's, let. A. vig. two females. "The Bank" &c., is spelt THE BANK. Paper thin.
10's, altered from 5's—the word TEN on the left border is on a WHITE ground—in the genuine it is on a BLACK.

Farmers' & Planters' Bank, Baltimore,.... ½
[Wm. E. Mayhew, Pres., T. B. Rutter, Cash.]
5's & **10**'s, spurious, said to be from genuine plates; name of the President is printed CHASTON instead of Cheston.
10's, altered from 1's—X on left hand margin.
50's, altered from 1's or 2's.

Fell's Point Savings Inst., Baltimore,........ 3

Franklin Bank of Baltimore,.............. ½
[J. J. Donaldson, Pres., A. P. Giles, Cash.]
1's, observe scratches over the goddess of liberty intended for rays, they look too heavy. The bill is well done.
☞ This bank failed some time since, and the old issue of genuine notes have almost all been redeemed.

Frederick County Bank, Frederick,.......... 1½
[John P. Thompson, Pres., H. Schley, Cash.]
10's, altered from 1's; vig. a female, bale of goods, &c.
10's, altered from 1's, and **20**'s, altered from 2's.

Hagerstown Bank, Hagerstown,............ do
[Alexander Neill, Pres., Elie Beatty, Cash.]
☞ Beware of bills of the Farm. & Millers Bank. At a first view they seem to read "Bank of Hagerstown."
1's, let. C'd, vig. a village, a bridge, and a stream.
3's, altered, from counterfeits of "Bank of Smyrna." A. Stockly, cash. Isaac Davis, pres. Filling up extremely bad.
5's, poorly done—word "Hagerstown" very crooked.
10's, paper of a blueish cast, the genuine is red.
10's, let. B. various dates, and pay to different persons. Paper of the counterfeit is of a blue tinge.

Havre de Grace Bank,....................(n) 2½
[Wm. Sappington, Pres., A. J. Austin, Cash.]

Marine Bank of Baltimore,.............. ½
[Jacob Bier, Pres., P. Littig, Jr. Cash.]
5's, lett. A, vig. steamboat, ship & sloop—Franklin on the right. Phil. Litting, Jr., Cash., J. Bier, Pres.; Mar. 5, 1839.
5's, let. C. pay M. Morris, April 4, 1826, J. Bier, Cash.
5's, lett. A. of a new emission, Oct. 14, 1826.
10's, lett. A. pay W. Hanson, Oct. 14, 1826.
100's, let. A. pay G. C. Miller—little smaller than genuine notes—the letter M in "MARINE," begins a little distance from the vignette; in the genuine notes it touches it.

Mechanics' Bank, Baltimore.................. do
[John B. Morris, Pres., Jas. W. Allnutt, Cash.]
2's, May 6, 1843, S. D. Day, Cash., N. Bishop, Pres.
5's, fraud. Vignette a ship under sail.
5's, spurious. vig. Neptune in a car; right end a steamboat, &c.; on left denomination of bill.
5's, vig. a female—Rawdon, Wright & Hatch, engravers.
5's, lett. B. pay to B. Stoddart, Dec. 20, 1815.
10s, alt'd, vig. a female, &c. W. Adams, H. H. Ellis, officers.
10's, lett. A.; vignette, n rail road.
10's, vig. a blacksmith, sledge & anvil, railroad cars in the distance—has but seven division-lines in the globe at the bottom, where the eagle rests—genuine has eight lines.
20's, let. A, the knuckles of the hand round the tomahawk are seen in the genuine, but not in the counterfeit.

Merchants' Bank, Baltimore,.................. do
[James Swan, Pres., Danl. Sprigg, Cash.]
2s, vig. Mercury on the left, reapers on the right, with "real estate pledged & private property holden," between signatures.
2's, counterfeit—has 17 dots on the upper end of the border. The genuine bill has sixteen.
2's. altered from a broken concern; "Baltimore" and "Maryland" inserted—vig. different from the genuine.
3's, vig. locomotive and cars; bull's head on the right.
5's, let. A. vig. two figures, one standing and one sitting. Paper white, filling and signing poor.
10's, altered from 1's. & read in the form of a certificate.
10s, an alteration, vig. female drawn in a car by seahorses.
10s, vig. a blacksmith with hammer, &c.
20s, spurious—vignette a blacksmith at his forge.

Mineral Bank, Cumberland,.................. 2
[Chas. M. Thruston, Pres., J. H. Tucker, Cash.]

Patapsco Bank, Ellicott's Mills.............. 1½
[T. B. Dorsey, Pres., B. U. Campbell, Cash.]

Plant. Bank of Prince George Co........worthless
Somerset & Worcester Bank, (and Branches). Broke
Susquehannah Bridge Co., Point Deposit,.....Broke
Susquehannah Bank,....................worthless

Union Bank of Maryland, Baltimore,...... ½
[J. M. Gordon, Pres., R. Mickle, Cash.]
2's, altered from the broken Globe Bank, N. Y.
5's, lett. D. pay different persons, various dates.
50's, lett. C. pay to S. Etting, May 2, 1812. President's name appears to be engraved.

Washington Co. Bank, Williamsport,...... 1½
[J. R. Dall, Pres., J. Van Lear, Jr. Cash.]
10's, let. A. vig. an eagle—on the right a woman and Indian, on the left a cupid and Washington.

Western Bank, Baltimore...................... ½
[Chauncey Brooks, Pres., J. H. Carter, Cash.]
5's, let. C., July 5, pay H. Taylor, Thos. Spencer, jr. cash. Sam. Jones, pres—well done. Others, Jan. 1, 1839, pay T. E. Hamblelod.
10's, altered from notes of 10th Ward Bank, N. Y.
20's, let. A, altered from the 10th Ward Bank, N. Y. vignette, a blacksmith, &c.

DIST. OF COLUMBIA.

Bank of Alexandria,......................worthless
Bank of Columbia, Georgetown,..........worthless

Bank of the Metropolis, Washington,........ 1
[John W. Maury, Pres., Richard Smith, Cash.]
3's, Jan. 1, 1815, Kerr, Cash., Van Ness, Pres.
5's, dated March 1, 1833, pay to C. Hill.

Bank of Potomac, Alexandria,................ do
[Phineas Janney, Pres., W. C. Page, Cash.]

Bank of Washington, Washington,.......... do
[Wm. Gunton, Pres., James Adams, Cash.]

Central Bank of Georgetown,............worthless

Farm. Bank of Alexandria, Alexandria,.... 1
[Robt. Jamieson, Pres., John Hooff, Cash.]
5's, let. B. pay John Jay, Nov. 5, 1821.
10's, let. D. pay John Jay, Nov. 5, 1821.
10's, let. A. pay Simon Bolivar, March 22, 1826.

Farmers' & Mech. Bank, Georgetown,...... do
[John Kurtz, Pres., Alex. Suter, Cash.]

Franklin Bank, Alexandria,................worthless
Mechanics' Bank, Alexandria,..............worthless
Merchants' Bank, Alexandria,..............worthless

Patriotic Bank of Washington, Wash'ton, 1
[Geo. C. Grammer, Pres., C. Bestor, Cash.]
100's, particulars unknown.

Union Bank of Georgetown, Georgetown,.... do
5's, lett. B. pay B. Stoddart, Dec. 29, 1815.

Washington Bank, Georgetown,..........worthless

VIRGINIA.

Bank of the Valley, Winchester,............ 1½
[Tho. Allen Tidball, Pres., H. M. Brent, Cash.]

Branch at Charleston,	*Cato Moore, Cash.*
Branch at Leesburg,	*Wm. A. Powell, Cash.*
Branch at Romney,	*John M'Dowell, Cash.*

1's, let. A. Jno. McDowill, cash., instead of McDowell.
3's, let. A. May 11, 1838, J. McDowell. cash., David Gibson, pres. Appearance bad.
5's, let. A. May 11, 1838, J. McDowell, cash, David Gibson pres. All notes over $3, are signed by the Cashier and Pres.
20's, vig. a figure of Mercury and a ship under sail.
20's, let. H. May 1, 1833, pay J. M. Broome.
20's, let. H. Sept. 14, 1838, pay J. Wood. H. M. Blunt, cash., Obed Waite, pres.
100's, let. A. pay in Romney, May 21, 1816.

Bank of Virginia, Richmond,................. 1½
[James Caskie, Pres., Saml. Marx, Cash.]

Branch at Fredericksburg,	*Wm. J. Roberts, Cash.*
Branch at Buchannan,	*J. Anthony, Cash.*
Branch at Charleston,	*Samuel Hannah, Cash.*
Branch at Danville,	*C. B. Taliaferro, Cash.*
Branch at Lynchburg,	*John M. Otey, Cash.*
Branch at Norfolk,	*Robt. W. Bowden, Cash.*
Branch at Petersburg,	*G. W. Steinback, Cash.*

5s, vig. a female, anchor, &c.—engraving dim.
5's, let. B. pay at Richmond, to L. Burfoot, Nov. 3, 1830, A. Robinson, cash.
5's. of Lynchburg Branch, pay —— Norvell, J. Brockenbrough, pres., W. Dandridge, Cash., 1819.
5's, of Charleston Branch, J. Brockenbrough, pres., A. Robinson, cash. Without No. or letter.
5's, let. C. pay at Danville, to Geo. Young.
5's, **10's** and **20's**, spurious, pay at different branches. The paper is of a whiter cast than genuine. The true 20's have a small flourish over letter K, in the word BANK, not to be found in the counterfeits.
10's, let. B, on various branches, vig. a female holding a child the child is scarcely discernible. The die work around the "TEN" and on the ends is bad.
10's. let. D. pay to W. B. Lamb, March 9, 1830. Signatures engraved. Pay at Norfolk.
10's, pay Geo. Towner, at Danville, Richmond, June 4, 1831, C. Robinson, cash., J. Brockenbrough, pres. Paper thin, vignette poorly engraved. General appearance bad.
10's, Petersburg Branch, July, 1832, pay John F. May—J. Brockenbrough, pres., W. Dandridge, cash.
10's, let. A. pay R. Gray, Richmond, Feb. 19, 1819.
10's, let. D. pay at Lynchburg, to Wm. Radford, Richmond, Sept. 22, 1819, and other dates. Wm. Nekervis, cash., P. N. Nicholas, pres.
10's, lett. unk., pay R. Gray, April 2, 1825.
10's, lett. B. pay J. Clark, Dandridge, Cash.
10's, let. B. pay at Richmond, to W. Billing, Feb. 23, 1819, Dandridge, cashier, Brockenbrough, president.
20's, let. D. pay in Norfolk, to Geo. Newton.
20's, let. B. pay at Lynchburg, to Jno. Early, president thereof, Richmond, March 2, 1819.
20's. The words, "Bank of Virginia," are on the right hand, instead of the left; the word "Twenty" is on the left, instead of the right.
20's, let. D. pay at Norfolk, to R. S. Leo.
20's, pay at Petersburgh, to J. F. May,
50's, altered from 5's, lett., date, &c. unknown.

Exchange Bank of Virginia, Norfolk,.... 1½
[Wm. W. Sharp, Pres., W. Southgate, Cash.]

Branch at Clarkesville,	*A. O. Finley, Cash*
Branch at Petersburg,	*P. Durkin, Cash.*
Branch at Richmond,	*Wm. P. Strother, Cash.*

3s, vig. three females and a ship, Atlas with globe on the left end, and a lady on the right.
5's, vig. several vessels, Washington on the left—has the words "States interest one moiety," on left upper corner.
5's, let. B—a close imitation of the genuine.
5's, vig. one vessel; the genuine has several.
20's, proof sheets, stolen from the engravers, dated previous to Sep. 1, 1838, at which time the bank went into operation.

Farmers' Bank of Virginia, Richmond,... 1½
[W. H. Macfarland, Pres., J. G. Blair, Cash.]

Branch at Charlotteville,	*Wm. A. Bibb, Cash.*
Branch at Danville,	*Geo. W. Johnson, Cash.*
Branch at Farmville,	*A. Vaughan, Cash.*
Branch at Fredericksb'g,	*Hugh M. Patton, Cash.*
Branch at Lynchburg,	*Alex. Tompkins, Cash.*
Branch at Norfolk,	*R. H. Chamberlain, Cash.*
Branch at Petersburg,	*Pleasant C. Osborne, Cash.*
Branch at Winchester,	*Jos. H. Sherrard, Cash.*
Branch at Wytheville,	*T. J. Morrison, Cash.*

5's, let. K—payable at Lynchburg, to Wm. Reading, April 6, 1833—signatures bad.
5's, let. L, pay at Lynchburg, filling up bad. Others, let. A. Easily detected.
5's, let. D. pay to B. Cooper, April 2, 1832.
5's, purports to be engraved by Murray, Draper, Fairman & Co., and printed on thin paper. The true 5's engra'd by Draper, Fairman & Co., are on thick paper.
5's, let. L. new plate, pay at Petersburg, to Wm. Robertson, Jr. filling up engraved, Nov. 4, 1827.
10's, let. A, June 13, 1838—N. Nichols, pres.; W. Wilkins, cash—new plate, no attempt to imitate.
10's, let. A. pay C. Greenleaf; a sheaf of wheat & a steam engine near the top, on the right. Others, pay W. Greenleaf, Indian female sitting on a rock, ship in the background.
10's, pay John T. Brooke, at Fredericksburg, Febr. 4, and Nov. 2, 1819—letter D.
10's, let. D, Jan. 11, 1841, pay W. Radford; engraving coarse and signing poor. Others, Jan. 1, 1841 payable at Lynchburg. Others, let. D; various dates.
10's, pay Daniel Lee, Winchester, Sep. 12, 1819.
10's, let. E. pay at Richmond, to C. Gerard, June 1, 1832. Others C. Geyega, various dates.
20's, let. A—vig. a female reaper—paper pale, filling up and signing appear to be done by one hand.
30's, counterfeit, the toes of the female in the vignette are visible in the genuine, but not in the counterfeit.
30's, altered from 5's, branch plate, letts. E F G or H. Figure 5 and word Five are extracted, and figures 30, and word Thirty stamped in their place.
50s, vig. a man under a tree, and a female at each end.
50s, let. B, vig. a farmer, sheaf of wheat, &c., dated at Richmond, April 4, 1840. Do not depend on the filling up.
50's, altered from 5's; have heads of Washington & Jefferson on them—the genuine 50s have not. Pay at Richmond.
50's, let. F. pay B. Hassey, Richmond, April 2.
50's, let. H. pay W. Radford, at Lynchburg, Sept. 2, 1827.
50's, let. A. pay at Lynchburg, Dandridge, pres.
100's, let. D. pay Wm. Clarke, Petersburg, April 2, Wm. Nekervis, cash., Benjamin Hatcher, pres.—well executed.
100's, letts. D & A, pay at Lynchburg branch, to Wm. Radford, April 2, 1818.

Merch. and Mech. Bank, Wheeling,....... 2½
[J. Caldwell, Pres., S. Brady, Cash.]

Branch at Morgantown, *W. Wagner, Cash.*

☞ Beware notes of this Bank, made payable at the Farmers & Mech. Bank of Philadelphia. They are forgeries.
5's, imperfect and rough; cashier's name engraved; the flourish around the letter "K" in "Bank," in the true notes touches the margin of the medallion head on the right end; in the counterfeit it lacks one-twelfth of an inch.

Monongahela Farmers' Company,.....worthless

North West'n Bank of Virginia, Wheeling, 2½
[Archibald Woods, Pres't, J. List, Cash.]

Branch at Wellsburg, *S. Jacob, Cash.*

10's, vig. agricultural implements and steamboat in the distance. Pay A. Williams.
10's, let. A, vig. an Indian, dog, and stag—on the right a steamboat, on the left a female. The genuine has a female with her arm resting on an anchor, with a ship, &c. for a vig.

Va. Salina Bank, Clarksburg,...............worthless
Western Bank of Va., Parkersburg,........worthless

NORTH CAROLINA.

Bank of State of North Carolina, Raleigh, 2½
[D. Cameron, Pres., Charles Dewey, Cash.]

Branch at Charlotte,	*Wm. A. Lucas, Cash.*
Branch at Elizabeth City,	*J. C. Ehringhaus, Cash.*
Branch at Fayetteville,	*I. Wetmore, Cash.*
Branch at Milton,	*Wm. R. Hill, Cash.*
Branch at Morgantown,	*Isaac T. Avery Cash.*
Branch at Newbern,	*John M. Roberts, Cash.*
Branch at Tarboro',	*P. P. Lawrence, Cash.*
Branch at Wilmington,	*W. E. Anderson, Cash.*

☞ Beware of the notes which read, "State Bank of North Carolina." They are worthless.
4s, imitation of genuine—engraving rather coarse.
4's, counterfeit, let. A; have a yellowish appearance—is a lithograph engraving, and blurred.
10's, vig. a female and sailor.

Bank of Cape Fear, Wilmington,............ 2½
[Thos. H. Wright, Pres., H. R. Savage, Cash.]

Branch at Asheville, *J. F. E. Hardy, Cash.*
Branch at Fayetteville, *John W. Wright, Cash.*
Branch at Raleigh, *W. H. Jones, Cash.*
Branch at Salem, *J. H. Lash, Cash.*
Branch at Salisbury, *D. A. Davis, Cash.*
Branch at Washington, *Benjamin Runyon, Cash.*

20's, let. A, pay S. Jewett, Feb. 1, 1846; vig. rail cars and mountain in distance; the heads on the ends very imperfect.

☞ There are various counterfeits on the old plates of this bank, dated previous to 1820; but none to our knowledge of a more recent date.

Bank of Newbern,........................worthless

Commercial Bank, Wilmington,.............. 2½

Merchants' Bank, Newbern,................ do
[Chas. Slover, Pres., Wm. W. Clark, Cash.]

State Bank of N. Carolina, Raleigh,....worthless

SOUTH CAROLINA.

☞ 1, 2 and 3 dollar notes,....... 4

Bank of Camden, Camden,................. 2½
[Wm. E. Johnson, Pres., W. J. Grant, Cash.]
5's, spurious, M. Maxwell, Pres., M. Johnson, Cash. The true bills have W. J. Grant, and W. M. Willie.

Bank of Charleston,........................ do
[H. W. Conner, Pres., Arthur G. Rose, Cash.]
Do do Payable in New-York,....... par
8s, this bank has no genuine bills of this denomination.
20's, let. A. vig. an eagle, on the right upper corner—goddess of liberty on the left. Filling up in a boy's hand.
20's, vig. railroad & mountain scene—not like genuine.
20's, let. A; pay at the Bk. of State of N. Y.; has the letter A in two places; the genuine has it only on the upper left end corner.
20's, let. C, poor paper, appearance light. The engraving is coarse, and the filling up poor.
50's counterfeit; payable in New-York.
50's, vignette at the bottom of the bill partly left out, likewise the names of the engravers.

Bank of Georgetown, Georgetown,........... 2½
[D. L. M'Kay, Pres., J. G. Henning, Cash.]
20s, vig. view of U. S. Bank, Philad. engraving coarse.
50's, vig. railroad & cars, arms of State below, lady and eagle on the right and the word "fifty" on the left, with Lafayette and Washington on the ends.

Bank of Hamburgh,........................ do
[H. Hutchinson, Pres., J. J. Blackwood, Cash.]

Bank of South Carolina, Charleston........ do
[Wm. Birnie, Pres., Geo. B. Reed, Cash.]
20's, letter, date, &c. unknown.

Bank of State of S. Carolina, Charleston,... do
[F. H. Elmore, Pres., C. M. Furman, Cash.]
Branch at Camden, *D. L. Desaussure, Cash.*
Branch at Columbia, *John Fisher, Cash.*
2s, let. E. March 11, 1811; signatures rather well done, engraving coarse, impression light, and paper poor.
2s, of Camden branch—engraving and signing very poor. Different dates—some payable to John Cant.
10's, altered from 1s; 4 ships between the portraits of Calhoun & Jefferson, slightly defective where altered.
10's, vig. a human figure betw'n the denominations. "S" in "dollars" is not right—"10" is also defective.
100's, altered from 2's, vig. an eagle—"TWO" & "2" have been extracted & those of ONE HUNDRED inserted.

Charleston Rail Road, Charleston,........... do

Cheraw Bank,...............................worthless

Commercial Bank, Columbia,................. 2½
[John A. Crawford, Pres., Benj. D. Boyd, Cash.]
10's, spurious, vig. steamboat; left end Vulcan. J. A. Crawford, pres., A. McLaughlin, cashier.
20's, altered from Commercial Bk Millington, Md.
50's, J. Ewart, cash. Mr. E. never was cashier. The name of A Blanding, pres. not like the genuine.

Merchants' Bank, Cheraw,.................. do
[Jas. Wright, Pres., W. Godfrey, Cash.]

Planters' & Mechanics' Bank, Charleston, do
[Danl. Ravenel, Pres., S. T. Robinson, Cash.]
5s, two infant figures, &c., on the left end.
5s, let. C. pay H. Morris. Looks like a wood cut.
5's, old plate, names of officers engraved.
10's, let. B, the "a" in "Bank," is only partially shaded—on the upper right end of the genuine, over the denomination, are 18 white dots, the counterfeit has 19.
20's. lett. ... pay A. Spears, Sept. 4, 1824.
20's, old plate, signatures of officers engraved.
50's let. D. Sept. 4, 1823, T. Blackwood, pres.
100's, let. D. Sept. 4, 1823, D. Ravenal, cash.
100's, let. H. pay M. G. Gibbs, Jan. 12, 1818.

South Carolina Railroad Script,.......... 2½
☞ These notes are signed James Gadsden, pres't.

South Western R. R. Co., Charleston,........ do
[Jas. Rose, Pres., James G. Holmes, Cash.]
Do do pay at Knoxville, Tenn............3
100's, vig. a railroad; genuine has a ship under sail.

State Bank of S. Carolina, Charlestown,....... 2½
[E. Sebring, Pres., Samuel Wragg, Cash.]
50's, let. D. pay E. Hurry, S. Wragg cash., T. Lee, pres. Others pay J. Jewry or bearer, Wm. Lee, pres.
100's, altered from 2's; hold them to the light.

Union Bank of S. Carolina, Charleston,.... do
[H. Ravenel, Pres., A. C. Smith, Cash.]

GEORGIA.

☞ 1, 2 & 3 dollar notes,........................ 4

Augusta Ins. & Bank'g Co., Augusta,...... 2½
[Wm. M. D'Autignac, Pres., R. Walton, Cash.]

Augusta Bridge Company,...............worthless

Bank of Augusta, Augusta,................ 2½
[- J. W. Davies, Cash.]
10's. old plate, vig. waggon & team; names engra'd.

Bank of Brunswick, (removed to Augusta.).... 3
[Edward Thomas, Pres., John Craig, Cash.]
Agency at Columbus, T. G. Casey, agent.

Bank of Milledgeville,...................... do
[Seaton Grantland, Pres., T. H. Hall, Cash.]

Bank of Darien, and branches,..............worthless

Bank of Macon,.............................worthless

Bank of the State of Georgia, Savannah,.... 2½
[Geo. B. Cumming, Pres., A. Porter, Cash.]
Branch at Athens, *Ashbury Hull, Cash.*
Branch at Augusta, *Isaac Henry, Cash.*
Branch at Eatonton, *D. R. Adams, Cash.*
Branch at Washington, *A. L. Alexander, Cash.*
20's, **50**'s & **100**'s, altered from 1's & 2's.
20's, let. K. pay S. Hall, Savannah, A. Porter, cash.
20's, pay S. Hale, Augusta, Oct. 27, J. Porter, cash.

Bank of St. Mary's, Columbus,................ do
[J. G. Winter, Pres., Geo. W. Winter, Cash.]
☞ This bank was formerly located at St. Mary's, & some of its notes in circulation are dated there.
The **25** Cent, **50** Cent & **75** Cent notes issued by this bank are good at 3 per cent discount.

Belfast Mining Co., and branch,............worthless

Central R. R. & Banking Co., Savannah,.. 2½
[R. R. Cuyler, Pres., Geo. J. Bullock, Cash.]

Cattahoochie R. R. & Bkg. Co.,..........worthless

Central Bank, Milledgeville,......................closed
Columbia Bank, Columbus,..................worthless
Commercial Bank, Macon,..................... —
[B. H. Moultree, Pres., A. Fleming, Cash.]
Farm. Bank at Cattahoochie,..........worthless

Georgia R. R. & Banking Co., Augusta,.. 2½
[John P. King, Pres., John W. Wild, Cash.]
Branch at Athens,

Hawkinsville Bank,........................ —

Marine & Fire Insur. Bank, Savannah,.. 2
[E. Padelford, Pres., Jona. Olmstead, Cash.]
Agency at Macon, *J. C. Plant, agent.*
10s, altered from genuine twos; hold them to the light.

Mechanics' Bank, Augusta..................... do
[A. Sebley, Pres., Milo Hatch, Cash.]

Merchants' Bank, Macon,..................(D.) —
[H. H. Turner, Pres., C. F. Smith, Cash.]
Merch. & Planters' Bank, Augusta,......worthless
Monroe R. R. & Banking Co., Macon,....worthless
Ocmulgee Bank, Macon,....................worthless

Planters' Bank, Savannah,..................... 2
[Goe. W. Anderson, Pres., H. W. Mercer, Cash.]
50's, let. C. pay P. Geurard or bearer, Feb. 1, 1813. Letter L. (for 50) on the right and left of the note.

Phenix Bank, Columbus,....................worthless
Planters & Mech. Bank, Columbus,......worthless

Ruckersville Banking Co., Ruckersville..... —
Western Bank, Rome,.......................worthless

ALABAMA, LOUISIANA and OHIO.   27

ALABAMA.

Bank of Mobile, Mobile,...................... 2½
[Wm. R. Hallett, Pres., Thos. M. English, Cash.]
10's, lithograph—the shading is wanting under the "F," in "Bank of"—commas in the engravers' names, are also omitted. Others, let. C, No. 416, Nov. 29, 1843.

Bank of the State, and Branches,............ 6
☞ This bank is winding up. Its large bills can be sold from 1 to 2 per cent better than we quote them.
20's, 50's, & 100's, altered from 2's, & 5's.
5's, from various branches. Engraving poor.
50's, spurious. They read "STATE BANK," &c.
100's, Dec. 20, 1820, pay to W. Tate.

Planters & Merch. Bank, Mobile...(Closing,) —

LOUISIANA.

Atchafalaya B. R. & Banking Co.,....worthless

Bank of Louisiana, New-Orleans,............ 2½
[Benjamin Story, Wm. E. Leverich, Cash.]
5's, altered from a broken bk., "Louisiana" defective.
50's, NEW PLATE, altered from 5's.
500's, let. A, on the right, Liberty with a shield; on the left, machine & circle. Leveritt, cash., Story, pres.
500's, let. A., Nov. 1, 1839; vig. Cybele & Mercury; on the right an Indian—bank has issued nothing like it.

Bank of Orleans,.................................closed

Canal and Banking Co., New-Orleans,..... 2½
[Glendy Burke, Pres., N. N. Wilkinson, Cash.]
5's, OLD PLATE, and the signatures well imitated.

Carrollton R. R. & Banking. Co., N.O.,... do

Citizens' Bank of Louisiana,...............closed

City Bank of New-Orleans, New-Orleans,.. 2½
R. J. Palfrey, Cash.]
50's, dated 12th March, 1832, S. J. Peters, pres., Richard Clague, cash. Badly executed.
100's, altered from 5's & 10's, payable at the Union Bank. New-York.

Clinton & Port Hudson R. Road Co.....worthless

Consolidated Association,....................closed

Exchange & Banking Co., N. Orleans........closed

Gas Light & Banking Co., N. Orleans,...... 2½
J. W. Houston, Cash.]

Improvement & Banking Co.............worthless

Louisiana State Bank, New-Orleans,........ 2½
R. Relf, Cash.]
10's, L. Bibl,-cash., C. Clement, prest. Engraved by the "WESTERN BANK NOTE COMPANY."
50's, spurious, M. S. Cucullu, pres. Sept. 8, 1830.

Mech. & Traders' Bank, New-Orleans,...... do
Samuel C. Bell, Cash.]
10's, filling up in boy's hand, very bad—officers both in same hand, in blue ink. Engraving rather coarse.
100's, altered from 10's. Very well done.

Merchants' Bank, New-Orleans,...........worthless

Planters' Bank of New-Orleans,........worthless

Union Bank of Louisiana, New-Orleans,.... 2½
F. Frey, Cash.]

OHIO.

Bank of Circleville, [Old Bank,]............. 3
[J. Olds, Pres., H. Lawrence, Cash.]
☞ All genuine notes are signed H. Lawrence, cash.

Bank of Chillicothe, Chillicothe,.............closed
Bank of Cincinnati,........................worthless
Bank of Cleveland, Cleveland,..............closed
Bank of Columbiana, N. Lisbon,...........closed
Bank of Gallipolis,.........................worthless
Bank of Geauga, Painesville, (Indp't)......... 3
[Daniel Kerr, Pres., John R. Finn, Cash.]
Bank of Hamilton, Hamilton,................closed
10's, paler than genuine, paper flimsy.
Bank of Mansfield,.........................worthless

Bank of Massillon, Massillon,................. 3
[Chas. K. Skinner, Pres., P. Handy, Cash.]
1's, let. A., pay bearer, poorly done.
10's, vig. a steamboat, ship & a sloop—TEN in separate circles; head of Daniel Webster on the end.

Bank of Marietta, Marietta,.................closed
3's, let. A. July 21, 1836—has a period at the word dollars —in the genuine there is none.
3's, let. A. dated April 1, 1837, pay to J. Nye, signed A. Nye cash., John Mills, pres.

Bank of Mount Pleasant,.....................closed

Bank of Norwalk, Norwalk,................... 3
[B. Higgins, Pres., Jas. D. Whitney, Cash.]
3., let. A. new plate, pay D. W. Darney, (engraved,) officers names are well executed. Engraving coarse.
10's, altered from the Bank of Vernon, Texas. John Gardner, cash., E. Lane, pres.

Bank of Sandusky, Sandusky................ do
[M. Burton, Pres., W. W. Wetherill, Cash.]
1's, purport to be engraved by Underwood, Bald & Spencer—genuine are by Casilear, Durand, Burton & Edmonds.
2's, let. B, vig. wolf and deer; lady on the left, sailor and anchor on the right. Officers' names in the same hand.—The bank, by its charter, is not permitted to issue twos.
3s, B. Higgins, pres., W. W. Wetherill cash.—pay O. Smith, 1844. No notes issued dated since 1842, and NONE payable to O. Smith. Rather pale, but well calculated to deceive.
5's, let. B, pay A. H. Barber, or bearer. The words "Five Dollars' in the body badly executed.
50's, let. A., well executed.
100's, let. A., various dates and filled up to different names—W. W. Witherell, cash.—bank has no 100's out.

Bank of Steubenville,.....................worthless
Bank of West Union,.......................worthless

Bank of Wooster, Wooster,.................... 3
[Geo. Wellhouse, Pres., O. Klemm, Cash.]
☞ Beware of notes on German Bank, which by scratching off "GERMAN," are made to read "Bank of Wooster."
1's, altered from Bank of Cincinnati; portrait of Harrison on left margin. Jos. S. Lake. cash., J. P. Coulton, pres.
3's, fac simile of genuine, engraving coarse; vig. goddess of agriculture and two Indians; Liberty on the right with a pole and cap. General appearance bad. Letter A.
3's, altered from ones—hold them to the light.
5's, spurious—vig. two Indians, with a steamboat in the distance. The Bank never issued such bills.
10's, J. S. Lake, cash., J. S. Coulter, pres., altered from fraudulent Bank of Vernon, Texas Vignette, two eagles, with shield of Hope; on right margin, shipping—on left, figure of a female, under which is the name of the engravers, Boston Bank Note Company, 39 State street. They do not resemble the genuine notes.

Bank of Xenia, Xenia,..................... closed

Bank of Zanesville, Zanesville,....(Closing,) 3
[Chs. G. Wilson, Pres., Chs. C. Gilbert, Cash.]
5's, let. A. pay to L. H. Dogan, 8th Feb. 1835, badly executed, paper thin, vignette defective. No period after the initial C. in the cashier's name.

Belmont Bank of St. Clairsville,..............closed

Butler County Bank,.......................worthless

Canal Bank, Cleveland,..................(Indp't) 3
[E. F. Gaylord, Pres., S. H. Mann, Cash.]

City Bank of Cincinnati,..................(Indp't) do
[L B. Headley, Pres., Lysle Lodwick, Cash.]

City Bank, Cleveland,....................(Indp't) do
[George Mygatt, Pres, W. H. Stanley, Cash.]

City Bank, Columbus,....................(Indp't) do
[Joel Buttles, Pres., Thos. Moodie, Cash.]

Clinton Bank, Columbus,..................... do
[Wm. S. Sullivant, Pres., D. W. Deshler, Cash.]
10's, altered from 2's, easily detected.

Commercial Bank, Cincinnati,......(Indp't) do
[Jacob Strader, Pres., James Hall, Cash.]
The genuine notes of the old bank of this name having been mostly all redeemed, it will be best to refuse all notes dated previous to 1845.

Comm. Bank of Scioto, Portsmouth,........closed
[J. E. Robinson, Pres., Henry Buchanan, Cash.]
☞ Bills of ALL denominations, on this bank, altered from broken Comm. Bank, Millington, Md.

Sou. Caro.
Georgia.
Alabama.
Louisiana
Ohio.

INDIANA.

Comm. Bk. of L. Erie, Cleaveland,............closed
  2's, let. A. Nov. 1, 1835, pay D. Mott, engraving and paper coarse—officers & style of engraving same as 5's below.
  5's, let. M. June 1, 1832, pay H. Dwight—very closely imitated—most striking difference is the signature of Cashier and filling up. T. P. Handy, cash. L. Case, pres.
  10's, Leonard Case, pres. T.P. Handy, cash. Too much uniformity in the writing.
  100's, let. A, Jan. 10, 1839. The bank has Issued no notes of this denomination of a later date than January 1837.

Dayton Bank, Dayton,................(Indep't)   3
  [J. Harshman, Pres., V. Winters, Cash.]
  The genuine notes of the old bank of this name having almost all been redeemed. It will be best to refuse all notes dated previous to 1845.
  5s, let. A, engraving poor; has no dot after DEMAND; letter A has no flourish like the N; in the genuine it has.
  5's, has two vignettes, one a lady, the other Henry Clay. A large 5 across the centre. Paper oily and flimsy.

Exch. Bk. & Sav. Inst., Cincinnati,........worthless
Farm. & Mech. Bank, Steuben'e,............closed
Farmers' Bank of Ashtabula, ..(Indp't)....   3
Farmers' Bank of Canton,.............worthless
Farmers' Bank of New Salem,.........worthless
Farm. & Mech. Bank, Chillicothe,......worthless
Farm. & Mech. Bank, Cincinnati,......worthless
Franklin Bank, Cincinnati,.....................   3
  The genuine notes of the old bank of this name have almost all been redeemed.
Franklin Bank of Zanesville, (Indp't)   do
  [D. Brush, Pres., John Peters, Cash.]
Farm., Mech. & Manuf., Chillicothe,......... fraud
Franklin Bank of Columbus,...............   3
  The genuine notes of the old bank of this name have almost all been redeemed.
German Bank of Wooster,.................. broke
Granville Alex. Soc., Granville,.............closed
Hamilton County Bank,................worthless
Hamilton & Rossville Manuf. Co......worthless
Jefferson Bank, New Salem,...........worthless
Kirtland Safety Society Bank,........worthless
Lafayette Bank, Cincinnati,....................   3
  [Gen. Carlisle, Pres., Wm. G. W. Gano, Cash.]
  1's, altered from plate of Cincinnati Loan Co.
  1's, counterfeit; vignette, a steamboat, "Ohio" on the wheelhouse. Indian on left end.
  3s, imitation of genuine—let. B. pay Wm. Willis—W. G. W. Gano, cash. G. Carlisle, pres.—Underwood, Bald, Spencer & Hufty, engra.—Declaration of Independence on the right—V on the head of Liberty, on the left.
  10's, let.—B. a fac simile of the genuine; the hat in the hand of Lafayette touches the letter "I" in Cincinnati; in the genuine it lacks a little of touching—engraving coarse
  10's, let B, exact copy of the genuine, but the engravin is very coarse, particularly the vignette.
  10's, let. B. paper thin, light coloured & greasy—vig. an eagle with wings extended, left side, a Cupid a stride a lion, purporting to be engraved by Woodruff and Hammond.
  100's, back plain; genuine has Lafayette Bank in red.
Lancaster Ohio Bank, Lancaster,...........closed
  5's, let. A. pay W. J. Reese, others pay S. Gill. All genuine notes which are payable to S. Gill, are numbered from 8000 to 9000, counterfeits are between 6000 and 7000. Those payable to W. J. Reese are numbered correctly.
Lebanon & Miami Banking Co.........worthless
Manhattan Bank,..........................worthless
Mech. and Traders, Cincinnati,........(closing) —
Miami Exp. Comp., Cincinnati,......(closed) —
Monroe Falls Manufac. Co...............worthless
Muskingum Bank, Putnam,............(Closing,) —
  [E. Buckingham, Pres. B. H. Buckingham, Cash.]
Ohio Life Ins. & Trust Co., Cincinnati,.....   3
  [Chs. Stetson, Pres., S. P. Bishop, Act. Cash.]
  [W. M. Vermilye, Cash. of the Co. & Agent in N.Y.]
  5's, let. B. H. Perkins, cash., W. T. Williams, pres. General appearance bad, more like lithograph than an engraving
Ohio R. R. Co., Richmond,..............worthless
Orphan Institute Bank, Fulton,.........worthless
Owl Creek Bank, Mount Vernon,.......worthless
People's Bank, Cincinnati,..........................
  [Peter B. Manchester, President,]
  ☞ This bank issues no bills, but its certificates of deposit are very prevalent. We have no confidence in it whatever.
Platt & Co.'s Bank, Cincinnati,..........worthless
Sandusky City Bank,..............(Indp'nt)   3
  [Wm. Townsend, Pres., S. W. Torrey, Cash.]
Seneca County Bank, Tiffin..........(indep'nt)   do
  [..............., Pres., W. E. Chittenden, Cash.]
State Bank of Ohio,..............................   do
  [G. Swan, Pres.,]
Akron Branch, Akron,
Belmont Branch, Bridgeport,
Chillicothe Branch, Chillicothe,   J. S. Atwood, Cash.
Commercial Branch, Toledo,   M. Johnson, Cash.

Commercial Branch, Cleveland,   T. P. Handy, Cash.
Dayton Branch, Dayton,   David Z. Peirce, Cash.
Delaware Co. Branch, Delaware,   B. Powers, Cash.
Exchange Branch, Columbus,   H. M. Hubbard, Cash.
Farmers' Bank, Salem,   John H. Ebbert, Cash.
Farmers' Branch, Munsfield.
Farmers' Branch, Ripley.
Franklin Branch, Cincinnati,   T. M. Jackson, Cash.
Franklin Branch, Columbus,   James Espy, Cash.
Hocking Valley Bank, Lancaster,   Wm. Slade, Jr. Cash.
Harrison Branch, Cadiz.
Jefferson Branch, Steubenville,   D. Moody, Cash.
Knox County Branch, Mount Vernon,
Lorain Branch, Elyria.   W. A. Adair, Cash.
Mad River Valley Br., Springfield,   J. T. Claypoole, Cash.
Marietta Branch, Marietta,   N. L. Wilson, Cash.
Mech. & Tra. Branch, Cincinnati,   S. S. Rowe, Cash.
Merchants' Branch, Cleveland,   Prentis Dow, Cash.
Miami County Branch, Troy,
Mt. Pleasant Branch, Mt. Pleasant.
Norwalk Branch, Norwalk,   John Gardiner, Cash.
Piqua Branch, Piqua.   Jas. G. Young, Cash.
Preble County Bank, Easton.
Portage County Branch, Ravenna,   E. Kinney, Cash.
Portsmouth Branch,   A. Spencer Nye, Cash.
Ross County Bank. Chillicothe.   A. Spencer Nye, Cash.
Summit Co. Bran., Cuyahoga Falls,   H. B. Tuttle, Cash.
Toledo Branch, Toledo,   T. S. Manley, Cash.
Union Branch, Massillon,
Wayne County Branch, Wooster,
Xenia Branch, Xenia.   E. F. Drake, Cash.
  100's, on the branches—none higher than 50s issued.
Stark Co. Orphan Inst. Canal, Fulton,....worthless
Urbana Banking Co., Urbana,.............closed

Western Reserve Bank, Warren,..(Indep't)   3
  [George Parsons, Pres., Geo. Taylor, Cash.]
  10's, old plate, letter D. Zalman Fitch, cash., Simon Perkins, Pres. "Western Reserve Bank" on the left, & "Ohio" on the right margin—on the genuine they are the reverse. Murray, Draper & Fairman's plate, badly executed.
Washington Bank, Miamisburgh,.........worthless
Western Reserve Farm. Bkg. Co.......worthless
Zanesville Canal & Manuf. Co..........worthless

INDIANA.

☞ 1, 2 and 3 dollar notes,........................   4
State Bank of Indiana, Indianapolis,........   3
  [James Morrison, Pres., James M. Ray, Cash.]
  ☞ The State Bank issues nor pays no notes except at its branches.

Branch at		
Indianapolis,	Thos. H. Sharp,	Cashier.
Lawrenceburgh,	Henry K. Hobbs,	do
Richmond,	Elijah Coffin,	do
Madison,	Joseph M. Moore,	do
New-Albany,	J. R. Shields,	do
Evansville,	George W. Rathbone,	do
Vincennes,	John Ross,	do
Bedford,	Isaac Rector,	do
Terre Haute,	Nathaniel Preston,	do
Lafayette,	Cyrus Belt,	do
Fort Wayne,	Hugh McCulloch,	do
South Bend,	Horatio Chapin,	do
Michigan City,	David Kriegh,	do

  1s, vig. winged females, with sword and scales—imitation of genuine, but poorly engraved. Notice the eyes.
  1s, vig. a figure of Justice—cashier's name engraved, and retouched with a pen.
  2's, let. E. vig. blacksmith shop; Cash'r and Pres't have no period;—the genuine have. Of the South Bend Branch.
  2's, let. B, Indianapolis branch; the figures "2" are not plain, in the genuine they are; the "T" & "w" in TWO join, in the genuine they do not touch. Pay H. Bates.
  2's, April 4, 1841, pay H. Bates, Thos. H. Sharp, ass't cash., O. Merrill, pres. Filling up and officers names engraved; the bill coarse & dark. Indianapolis branch.
  2's, let. D; A. P. Andrews, jr. cash., S. Merrill, pres. The imitation of the president's signature is good; paper thick & rough. Fulton's eyes (right end of note), much blurred.
  5's, vig. two females sitting on an iron chest, like most of the genuine notes: around the vig. are coarse straight lines, easily seen—on the genuine they are very perfectly clouded.
  5's, pay at the Madison branch, to H. Watts; signatures are apparently in the same hand; in the genuine note the female's adress is plain and distinct, in the counterfeit it is blurred, and without proper shade.
  5's, lets. AA, vig. cradles—heads of Washington & Lafayette on the ends—genuine have Franklin and Wayne
  5's, centre vig. a ship, which none of the genuine have. The name of Merrill is engraved.
  5's, let. D. vig. a woman and ship, with portraits of Washington & Lafayette rather dull, dead looking. Letter V, on left hand margin, is too narrow, and not well proportioned. They are made payable at the different branches.

5's, engrv'd by W.Dane&Co.—Rawdon,Wright& Hatch, or Draper,Toppan&Co. have done the engrav'g of the bank.

5's, vig. a female looking to the RIGHT, her arm resting on a sheaf of wheat, plough, &c. In the genuine the vig. is the same, but the female faces the LEFT, not the right.

5's, Jan.1,1839. Bank never issued bills dated Jan.1,1839.

10s, vig. an Indian viewing a train of cars; train of cars and lady and gentleman on the right, sheaf of grain on the left end. Paper and engraving poor. No genuine like this.

10's, let. A. vig. a naked figure sitting, a sailor, ship, &c. At the bottom is an Indian in a canoe; heads of Washington and Lafayette on the margins.

10's, vignette a view of a steamboat, ship, &c.

20's, May 1, 1839; R. Millikin, cash., S. Merrill, pres.; filled up to all the branches—well calculated to deceive.

20's, let. A. variously filled up and dated; paper lighter, note shorter, and engraving less distinct than genuine; lines of clouding around the State House are too coarse—the lathe work around the figures is not distinct.

20's& **100's**, altered from 5's, clumsily done, having retained the heads of particular individuals, as all the 5's have; none of which are on the genuine $20 or $100. The upper and lower margin is cut off in making the alteration.

100's, let. A. payable ninety days. Dated Mar. 4, 1843. Well executed, and calculated to deceive.

☞ A number of fraudulent notes are in circulation, ingeniously pieced & pasted together—hold them to the light, and the fraud may be discovered. Notes so pieced, should be refused, as the bank will not redeem them at full price.

ILLINOIS.

☞ *All the Banks in this State are worthless, except the following:*

Bank of Illinois, Shawneetown,........(closed) 75
[Winding up, David Prickett, Commissioner.]

☞ The bills of these TWO Banks having been mostly redeemed, we omit describing the counterfeits; it is best for those not well acquainted with them to reject all.

State Bank of Illinois, Springfield,............. 50
[Winding up, Norman H. Purple, Agent.]

KENTUCKY.

☞ 1, 2 and 3 dollar notes,........................ 3

Bank of Kentucky, Louisville,.................. 2½
[V. McKnight, Pres, G. C. Gwathmey, Cash.]

Branch at Lexington,	*Wm. S. Waller, Cash.*
Branch at Maysville,	*H. B. Hill, Cash.*
Branch at Frankfort,	*Edmund H. Taylor, Cash.*
Branch at Greenburg,	*Wm. B. Allen, Cash.*
Branch at Bowling Green,	*Richard Curd, Cash.*
Branch at Hopkinsville,	*Reuben Rowland, Cash.*
Branch at Danville,	*Thos. Mitchell, Cash.*

1's, No 4341, April 1, 1841—new bill—pay J. T. Sanders, at Louisville; filling up in blue ink; president's name engraved and retouched with black ink, paper flimsy and of a bluish cast. Engraving coarse.

2's, imitation of genuine, signatures engraved and retouched with a pen—pay to J.W.Hunt, and others.

3s, let. A. Engraving very coarse.

5's, let. B. variously fitted up; appearance tolerably good but paper bad.

5's, let. C. payable to John P. Campbell, of various dates, paper thin and dark.

5's, let. B; variously filled up—G. C. Gwathmey, cash., W. H. Pope, pres't; vig. a horse. In the genuine there is a perfect wreath surrounding the figure 5; in the spurious it is but partly formed. The bill is calculated to deceive.

10's, altered from 5's; vig. a horse, which is not on the true 10's—by which they can be detected.

20's, let. A. and others B. The figure of the Indian, on left end, is much lighter, and imperfect, particularly about the head. The word "bearer" is shorter, and the filling up badly done. It is poorly executed, being much too light.

50s, let. D, vig. a female and two boys; filling up and signing good—paper thin.

100's, post note, let. A. dated Jan. 1, 1840; G.C. Gwathmey, cash., V. M'Knight, pres. Signatures and filling up engraved. Payable to order of A. Akrir, and by him endorsed in a cramped hand.

100's, let. A., John J. Jacob, pres., G. C. Gwathmey, cash. Near ¼ of an inch shorter than the genuine; engraving dark; signatures engraved and inked over.

100's, let. B., G. C. Gwathmey, cash., W. K. Pope, pres.; vig. an eagle—on each end a female figure. Paper rather flimsy, but well calculated to deceive.

Bank of Louisville,.......................... 2½
[Josh. B. Bowles, Pres., A. Thurston, Cash.]

Branch at Paducah,	*Adam Rankin, Cash.*
Branch at Flemingsburg,	*H. Powers, Cash.*

1's, vig. a train of ears, with a steamer above; July 1843, J. S. Snead, pres. Mr. S. died long before this date.

1's, the true 1's are signed by the cashier, only.

3's, let. A. vig. a steamboat at the bottom of the note near the left end. A. Thurston, cash.

3's, the flourish over the K in the word BANK is omitted.

5's, let B. pay B. Rand of various dates; A. Thurston, cash., John S. Snead, pres.—badly done; vignette miserably engraved; the "a" in Draper & Bald, (the engravers' names,) is placed backwards.

10s, let. A. vig. a female, and a ship in the distance. The filling up in one handwriting—paper flimsy, impression light. This is on the Branch at Flemingsburg.

Commonwealth Bank,...................Worthless
Hotel Company,............................Worthless

Northern Bank of Kentucky, Lexington,.... 2½
[John Tilford, Pres., M. T. Scott, Cash.]

Branch at Covington,	*P. S. Bush, Cash.*
Branch at Louisville,	*W. Richardson, Cash.*
Branch at Paris,	*Thos. Y. Brent, Cash.*
Branch at Richmond,	*E. L. Shackelford, Cash.*

1's, the "o" in "N-o-rthern Bank of Kentucky" on the scroll held by a lady in the vig., is smaller than the other letters; and in "Ky." after Lexington, there is no dot (.) after the K and under the y, the genuine has a full period.

2's. let. B., Nov. 4, 1845—paper flimsy. The cashier's signature is lithographed; genuine is written with a pen.

3's, paper light, and engraving faint; otherwise calculated to deceive. M. T. Scott, cash.

5s, altered from ones—hold them to the light.

5's, let. E. pay Thomas Kelly, M. T. Scott, cash., John Tilford, pres.; filling up and signatures clumsy, and in one hand. The paper flimsy, and engraving faint.

5's, let. E. pay E.Smith; M.T.Scott, cash., John Tilford, pres. Engraving poor and paper dark and cloudy.

5's, let. E; pay W.Caperton, Mar. 9, 1840—paper coarse, thick and whitish, engraving cloudy; president's name too small a hand & too short—name of cashier engraved.

10's, let. A or C., the two "ll"s in "will" touch the line above, in the genuine they do not—bill appears blurred.

10's, let. A. vig. railroad train; engraving poor and light. These notes are ¼ of an inch too short.

20's, let. B. vig. railroad cars; M. T. Scott, cash., filling up in pale ink.

20's, let. E., well done—"Northern Bank of Kentucky," on the scroll held by a lady, is rather blurred & indistinct.

20's, the shading of the words "Northern Bank of Kentucky," is much darker and wider than in the genuine; the lines on the ends of the note crooked and irregular; engraving darker and coarser than the good note.

20's, let. D., variously filled up; M. T. Scott, cash., John Tilford, pres. "Twenty" nearly touches the right margin in the genuine; in counterfeit it is ¼ of an inch from it.

20's, spurious—vig. a man in a sitting posture with a female kneeling, (not on the genuine,) engraving coarse.

20's, let. A. May 1st, 1843, filling up well done; paper thin and poor.

20's, let. B., pay Thomas Kelly, Oct. 28, 1838; vig. a train of cars, poorly executed; engraving too dark; paper flimsy; M. T. Scott, cash., John Tilford, pres.

100's, let. B. pay to B. Moore; M. T. Scott, cash., John Tilford, pres. Vignette dark and imperfect.

100's, let. D., Nov. 10, 1842; M. T. Scott, cash.

TENNESSEE.

1, 2 & 3 dollar notes are 4 per cent discount

Bank of Tenn, Nashville, (and Branches,)..(D.) 5 to 8
[A.O.P.Nicholson, Pres., David Graham, Cash.]

Branch at Rogersville,	*H. Fain, Cash.*
Branch at Somerville,	*W. Houston, Cash.*

10's, let. A., 23d June, 1838; payable 12 months after date; whole appearance bad.

10's, let. A. dated April 9, 1839; Henry Ewing, cashier, (written "Euing,") M. Nichol, pres.

50's, altered from 10's—the coat of arms of the State is on the right centre; in the genuine it is on the left centre; the alteration has been made upon all the branches.

Farm. & Mech. Bank, Nashville,..........Worthless

Farmers' & Merch. Bank, Memphis,.....broke —
[Seth Wheatley, Pres., Charles Lofland, Cash.]

5's, a close imitation, though clumsily filled up.

100's, altered from 5's; easily detected.

Franklin & Fayetteville Bank,........Worthless

Planters' Bank of Tenn., Nashville,......(D.) 5 to 8
[M. Watson, Pres., Nicholas Hobson, Cash.]

Branch at Athens,	*David Clage, Cash.*
Branch at Clarksville,	*Wm. P. Hume, Cash.*
Branch at Franklin,	*Thos. Parks, Cash.*
Branch at Memphis,	*James Penn, Cash.*
Branch at Pulaski,	*E. B. Smith, Cash.*

10's, let. B. Nashville, June 1, 1845, paper poor and appearance rough. W. Watsod, pres, N. Ludlow, cash.

10's, dated twice; mechanics arm & hammer at bottom.

10's, 20's, 50's & 100's, genuine engraving of Rawdon, Wright & Hatch, obtained by fraud. They read "pay to the bearer on demand," the genuine read "pay to—— or bearer on demand."

100's, let. C; vig. a herd of deer, &c.; Washington on the right; engraving good, but not like the genuine.

MISSISSIPPI, MISSOURI, FLORIDA, ARKANSAS, MICHIGAN, CANADA, &c.

100's, let. A, vig. railroad cars, ste*mbonts, &c. pay A. Crawford; March 4, 1844; the shading of "Planters' Bank of Tennessee," very poor; engraving too dark ; the note is wider th n the genuine. Engraved by Rawdon, Wright, Hatch & Edson, New-Orleans; others, of same plate, payable at the different branches, are in circulation.

Union B. of Ten, Nashville, (and branches) (D.) 5 to 8
[John M. Bass, Pres., J. Correy. Cash.]

Branch at Knoxville,   Hugh A. M. White, Cash.
Branch at Jackson,   J. W. Campbell, Cash.

1s, paper & engraving poor—counterfeit signatures.
1s, let. A. vig. a female, steamboat. &c.—paper thin.
10s, let. A, vig female, steamboat, &c. Paper thin.
10's, alt'd from 1's; on ther ght end a figure representing Fame ; medallion head of Jackson on left; the genuine have (in centre) a female feeding an eagle from a goblet.
100's, altered from 5's; an eagle at each end. The genuine have a full length figure of Justice on each end.

MISSISSIPPI.

☞ All banks in this State are broken, and their notes are of doubtful and nominal value.

MISSOURI.

The following are the only good Banks in the State.

Bank of the State of Missouri, St. Louis,.... 3
[Robt. Campbell, Pres., H. Shurlds, Cash.]

Branch at Fayette,   W. C. Boon, Cash.
Branch at Jackson,   T. B. English, Cash.
Branch at Lexington,   Wm. Limrick, Cash.
Branch at Palmyra,   S. D. South, Cash,
Branch at Springfield,   J. R. Danforth, Cash.

10's, genuine have "Ten Dollars," frequently repeated, at top & bottom—in the counterfeit "Dollar" is omitted.
10's, pay at St. Louis ; shorter than genuine; vig. a railroad ; genuine have a steamboat, with the words "Gen Pike" on the wheelhouse Paper white and coarse ; the name of the cashier engraved.
20's, pay to bearer, at Lexington; vig. a building with eight columns, surrounded by trees. Engraving coarse.

FLORIDA.

☞ All the banks in this State are broken and their notes are of doubtful and nominal value.

ARKANSAS.

☞ All the banks in this State are broken and their notes are of doubtful and nominal value.

TEXAS.

Commercial & Agricultural Bank, Galveston,
[Saml M. Williams, Pres., Jno. W. McMillen, Cash.]

MICHIGAN.

☞ We give below all the good Banks in this State, those not named are worthless.

Bank of Michigan, Detroit,.................. —
Bank of St. Clair, St Clair, ... broke
Bank of River Raisin, Monroe,............broke
[A E. Wing, Pres., N. R. Haskill, Cash.]
Farm. & Mech. Bk., Detroit,................ 4
[Chas. Seymour, Pres, E. C. Litchfield, Cash.]
Agency at Niles,   R. C. Paine, Cashier.
Michigan Insurance Co., Detroit,.......... du
[John Owen, Pres., H. H. Brown, Cash.]
Michigan State Bank, Detroit,.............. do
Oakland County Bank, Pontiac,......... fraud

WISCONSIN.

Wisconsin Ins. Co.'s (Checks,) Milwaukie,.... 3
☞ Beware of notes which read, "Marine and Fire Insurance Co.," of Grant county, Sinipee—they are frauds.

IOWA.

Miners' Bank, Dubuque,......................... —

CANADA.

☞ The following are the only good Banks in Canada.

Bank of British N. America, Quebec,...... 5
[Robert Cassels, Manager.]
Branch at Montreal,   David Davidson,   Manager.
"   Kingston,   Thos. Askew,   do
"   Toronto,   W. G. Cassels,   do
"   Hamilton,   J. Jaffray,   do
"   Dundas,   J. B. Ewart,   Agent.
"   Brantford,   J. Christie,   do
"   Port Hope,   David Smart,   do
"   Bytown,   A. C. Kelty,   do
New-York City, R. Bell, Wm. Machachlan, H.E. Ransom, Agts.

Bank of Montreal, Montreal,................. 5
[Hon. P. M'Gill, Pres., A. Simpson, Cash.]
Branch at Toronto,
Agency at Kingston, C. Miller, agent.
Agency in London, U. O., Mr. Fraser, agent

5's, Toronto Branch, let. A. pay Baker, the word VALUE to the left of TORONTO; in the genuine it is directly over "Toronto." In the counterfeit the nose of the small dog comes very near the T in "Toronto;" in the genuine it is ⅛ of an inch from the T.
5's, let. A. of Montreal Bank, pay cashier or bearer, 1st March, 1819.
5's, let. B. which read Montreal Bank, pay L Carlle in Quebec, April 2d, 1819.
5's, let. C. Montreal Bk, Oct. 2, 1821, pay W. Radenhaun.
5's, altered from—has a V, in a circle, at the bottom, substituted in place of a king's head on the ones.
5's, altered from 1's; vig. a female reclining on a figure 5, clumsily altered from the figure 1.
10's; pay to B. Holmes, Griffin, cash, Grey, pres.
10's, altered from 1's; vig. Brittannia with a spear and shield, and the head is placed after the signature of the cashier. The genuine 10's have a ship, and the words "Bank of Montreal" are in the line.

Bank of the People, Toronto,........(Closed,) do
10's, spurious, well done. There are ly a few genuine 10's out. and have John Rolph, as esident and. James Leslie, as ccashier.

Banque de Peuple, Montreal,................. do
[L. M. Viger, Pres., B. H. Le Moine, Cash.]
Branch at Quebec,

Bank of Upper Canada, Toronto,........... 3
[W. Proudfoot, Pres., Thos. G. Ridout, Cash.]
Branch at Montreal,
10's, altered from 1's. The true 10's have for a vignette a landscape view. True 1's, a bee hive.
10's, close imitation. let. C. 1st Nov. 1830, general appearance darker than the genuine, particularly in the fore-ground of the vig., and the figure X at the bottom.
20's, lett. A. pay B. Holmes, 10th Oct 1817; others, same lett. pay to McBlair, Jan. 1st, 1818.

City Bank, Montreal,............................
[J. Frothingham, Pres., Chas. H. Castle, Cash]

Commercial Bank, Midland District, Kingston, do
Branch at Montreal,
5's, spurious, vig. a female leaning on a wheel.
10's, altered—hold them up to the light.

Gore Bank, Hamilton,......................... do
Quebec Bank, Quebec,......................... do

NEW-BRUNSWICK.

Bank of Brit. N. Am., St. Johns,............ 6
Branch at Fredericton, J. Johnson, pro Acct.
Central Bank, Fredericton,................... de
[W. J. Bedell, Pres., Sam. W. Babbitt, Cash.]
Charlotte County Bank, St. Andrew,...... du
[Harris Hatch, Pres., J. Rodgers, Cash.]
Commercial Bank, St. Johns,................
[John Duncan, Pres.
Branch at Fredericton, A. Scott, Cash.
New-Brunswick Bank, St. Johns,........... de
[Thos. Leavitt, Pres., R. Whiteside, Cash.]
Saint Stephen Bank, St. Stephen,........... de
[D. Upton, Cash.]

NOVA SCOTIA.

Bank of Nova Scotia, Halifax,................ 6
Bank of Halifax,............................... do
Bank of the Province, Halifax,.............. do
Bank of British N. America, Halifax....... do
Halifax Banking Comp., Halifax............ do

THOMPSON'S REPORTER.

Rules to be observed in referring to this Bank Note List.

1st. The States are placed in geographical order, commencing with the custom.
2d. The name of the Bank is in full-faced type; the rate of discount is carried out to the end of the line.
3d. The letter (S.) attached to a bank indicates that the rate of discount is doubtful. The Safety Fund banks in the State of New York are designated by (S); the Free banks by (F). If a bank is dashed (—) it is worthless. If the name of a bank cannot be found in this list, do not take it.
4th. The names of the present President and Cashier, follow immediately under the Bank, and the description of counterfeits, altered notes, &c., follow next.
5th. The 1st page is devoted to money articles, statistics, &c., except when used for Mercantile Cards.
6th. Our quotations are made to correspond with the rates of doing business at our Exchange Office, 64 Wall st.; where every branch of a Money and Stock Broker's business is done, upon fair and honorable principles.

TABLE of GOLD COINS.

AMERICAN.
Eagles, ... since 1833 .... $10,00
Half-Eagles, ... since 1833 5,00
Quarter-Eagle, ... since 1833 2,50
Eagles, (old,) .... before 1834 11,50
Half-Eagles, (old,) .... before 1834 5,25
Quarter-Eagle, (old) before1834 2,62
Carolina & Geo. $5, of all dates (shares in prop.) 4,75

ENGLISH.
(a) Sovereigns, ... of all dates..... 5 dwt. 3 grs...$4,83
Half Sovereigns, ...of all dates..... 2 " 13 " .. 2,41
Guineas .... of all dates..... 5 " 7 " .. 5,00
English Gold, per act of Congress of March 3, 1843, is a legal tender at 94 cts. 6 mills per dwt.

SPANISH.
(b) Doubloons, ... all dates..... 17 dwt. 8 grs...$16,00
Half Doubloons .... all dates..... 8 " 16 " .. 8,00
Quarter Doubloon .... all dates..... 4 " 8 " .. 4,00
Eighth Doubloon .... all dates..... 2 " 4 " .. 1,87
Spanish Gold, per act of Congress of March 3, 1843, is a legal tender at 80 cents 9 mills per dwt.

FRENCH.
Napoleons, (20 franc,) .... of all dates..... 4 dwt. 3 grs. $3,83
2 Napoleons, (40 franc,) ...... of all dates..... 8 " 6 " 7,66
Louis d'or, ... of all dates..... 4 " 20 " 4,50
French Gold, per act of Congress of March 3, 1843, is a legal tender at 92 cts. 9 mills per dwt.

MEXICAN and SOUTH AMERICAN.
(b) Doubloons, ... all dates..... 17 dwt. 8 grs ...$15,55
Half Doubloons, ... all dates..... 8 " 16 " .. 7,75
Quarter Doubloon .... all dates..... 4 " 8 " .. 3,87
Eighth Doubloon .... all dates..... 2 " 4 " .. 1,87
Mexican & South American Gold, per act of Congress of March 3, 1843, is a legal tender at 89 cts. 9 mills per dwt.

PROMISCUOUS COINS.
Ten Thalers, ...alldates, (shares in pro.) 8 dwt. 10 grs. $7,80
Fr. d'or, of Denmark or Prus..........alldates,4 " 5 " 3,90
Double do. do. ....alldates,8 " 10 " 7,80
10 Guilder, (shares in propor.) ....alldates, 4 dwt. 7 grs. $4,00
(c) Johannese, John V.........(shares in pro.) 18 " 17 " 17,00
Moldore, (Brazilian)...................5 " 4 " 4,87
Ducat, (Netherlands, Denm'k, Prus.&c.,....2 " 5 " 2,20
Crown (Porig'l) Maria I I....(shares in pro.)6 " 4 " 5,80
Zervonitz, (Russia,).................... " 2 " 2,00
Xeriff, (Turkey,)........................2 " 7 " 2,30
Pistole, (Italy,)........................3 " 11 " 3,25

(a) The dragon sovereigns, so called, are worth only $4,80.
(b) Many doubloons and parts of doubloons are light, and consequently not saleable. A doubloon should weigh the same as a good dollar, or two half dollars.
(c) Most of the Johannese and half Joes now in circulation are light. They should be taken at the rate of 80 cents for the weight of a five cent piece.

Table of Silver Coins.

Spanish pillar dollars, (unblemished,) .... 2 per ct. pre.
Spanish halves, quarters, &c. .... par a ¼ dis.
Mexican dollars, ... ¼ a ½ prem.
Five franc pieces, ... 98 cents.
Two francs 35 cents, and One franc 17 cents.
French Crowns, ... 1,07
English Crowns $1,15; Half Crowns, 57 cts.
English Shillings, (sixpences in proportion) ..... 23 cents.
Thalers, ... 66 cents.
Pistoreens, (head,) .... 18 cents.
Pistoreens, (cross,) .... 16 cents.
One Gilder, ... 36 cents.
☞ Counterfeit Dollars (particulary Mexican) are in circulation, so well done as to pass through most hands without detection.

MISCELLANEOUS MATTER.

List of Country Banks par in N. Y.

		Where redeem.
Albany City Bank,	100's,	State Bank.
Albany Exch. Bank,	all,	Merch. Exch. Bank.
Bank of Albany,	50's & 100's,	Bank of New-York.
Bank of Newburgh,	all,	Merch. Exch. Bank.
Bank of Kinderhook,	all,	Amer. Exch. Bank.
Bank of Poughkeepsie,	all,	Merchants' Exch. Bk.
Bank of Troy,	50's & 100s,	Merchants' Bank.
Catskill Bank,	all,	Merch. Exch. Bank.
Commercial Bank Albany,	all,	Bank of Commerce.
Dutchess County Bank,	all,	Phœnix Bank.
Farmers' Bank Troy,	all,	Merchants' Bank.
Farmers' Bank of Hudson,	all,	Mechanics' Bank.
Farm. & Drov. Bank, Seneca,	all,	Merch. Exch. Bank.
Farm. & Manuf. Bk., Po'keepsie,	all,	Phenix Bank.
Hudson River Bank, Hudson,	all,	Leather Manuf. Bank.
Highland Bank, Newburgh,	all,	Phœnix Bank.
Kingston Bank, Ulster County,	all,	State Bank.
Merchants Bank, Po'keepsie,	all,	Phenix Bank.
Mech. & Far. B'k, Albany,	50's, 100's,	Merchants' Bank.
Powell Bank, Newburgh,	all,	Amer. Exch. Bank.
Prattsville Bank,	all,	Mechanics' Bank.
Tanners' Bank, Catskill,	all,	Amer. Exch. Bank.
Ulster County Bank,	all,	Merch. Exch. Bank.
Westchester County Bank,	all,	Merch. Exch. Bank.

New-Jersey Banks par in N. Y.

		Where redeem.
Belvidere Bank,	10's and over,	Merch. Exch. Bank
Commercial Bank,	10's and over,	Mechanics' Bank.
Far. & Merch. Bk. Mid. Pt.	5's & over,	Fulton Bank.
Far. & Mech. B k Railway,	10's & over,	Merchants' Bank.
Mech. Bank, Newark,	5's & over,	Mechanics' Bank.
Mech. & Manuf. Bk, Trenton,	5's and over,	Phenix.
Morris County Bank,	10's & over,	North River Bank.
Newark Insurance Co.,	5's & over,	Merchants' Bank.
Orange Bank,	5's and over,	Amer. Exch. Bank.
Sussex Bank,	10's and over,	Merch. Ex. Bank.
State Bank at Morris,	10's and over,	North River Bank.
State Bank at N. Bruns.	5's & over,	Phenix Bank.
State Bank at Newark.	5's & over,	Manhattan Bank.
State Bk. at Elizabeth,	5's & over,	Merchants' Bank.
Trenton Bk'g. Co.,	5's & over,	Manhattan Bank.

Miscellaneous.
Easton Bank, Pa., ... all, Union Bank.

List of Banks at par in Philadelphia.

All the Banks in the City of Philadelphia.
Bank of Chester County, at Westchester, Pa. .... All
Bank of Delaware County, at Chester, Pa. .... All
Bank of Germantown, Pa. .... All
Bank of Montgomery County, at Norristown, Pa. ...... All
Bank of Northumberland, Pa. .... All
Columbia Bank and Bridge Company, at Columbia, Pa. ...All
Doylestown Bank, Pa. .... All
Easton Bank, Pa. .... All
Farmers Bank of Bucks County, at Bristol, Pa. .... All
Farmers Bank of Lancaster, Pa. .... All
Farmers Bank of Reading, Pa. .... All
Farmers Bank of Schuylkill Co. at Schuylkill Haven, Pa.. All
Lancaster Bank, Pa. .... All
Lebanon Bank, Pa. .... All
Lancaster County Bank, at Lancaster, Pa. .... All
Miners Bank of Pottsville, Pa. .... All
Bank of Delaware, at Wilmington, Del. .... 5s & over
Bank of Smyrna, Del. .... 5s & over
Branch of same at Milford, Del. .... 5s & over
Wilmington and Brandwine Bank, at Wilmington. 5s & over
Farmers Bank of the State of Delaware, at Dover.. 5s & over
Branch of same at Wilmington, Del. .... 5s & over
Branch of same at Newcastle, Del. .... 5s & over
Branch of same at Georgetown, Del. .... 5s & over
Union Bank of Delaware, at Wilmington, Del. . 5s & over
Burlington County Bank, at Medford, N. J. ... 5s & over
Cumberland Bank of New-Jersey, at Bridgeton. 5s & over
Farmers Bank of New-Jersey, at Mount Holly.. 5s & over
Mechanics Bank of Burlington, N. J. .... 5s & over
Mechanics & Manufacturers Bank, at Trenton, N. J. 5s & over
Princeton Bank, N. J. .... 5s & over
Salem Banking Company, N. J. .... 5s & over
State Bank, at Camden, N. J. .... 5s & over
Trenton Banking Company, N. J. .... 5s & over

Mississip.
Missouri.
Florida.
Arkansas.
Michigan.
Wisconsin.
Iowa.
Canada.
N. Bruns.
Nov. Sco.

MISCELLANEOUS MATTER.

New Counterfeits.
2's, on the Merchants Bank, Ellery, N. Y. Page 17.
10's, on the Sussex Bank, New-Jersey. Page 20.
10's, on the Chemung Canal Bank. Page 10.
10's, on the Cayuga County Bank. Page 16.
3's, on the Commercial Bank of Oswego. Page 16.
5s, on the Champlain Bank. Page 16.
5's, on the Bank of Silver Creek, N. Y. Page 15.
1's, on the Randolph Bank, Mass. Page 6.
3's, on the Randolph Bank, Mass. Page 6.
5's, on the Bank of Commerce, Phil. Page 21.

Chart to Broken Bank Money.

JAMES' BANK.
Securities.   Circulation.
B. & Mortg. $15,943 $69,266
N.Y. 5 pr cts 8,290   From the proceeds of these se-
Do 5¼ do 6,000   curities, we estimate that the Con-
U.S. 5 pr cts 5,000   troller will pay 75 cents on the
Mich. 6 pr cts 18,000   dollar.
$63,143

ATLAS BANK.
Securities.   Circulation.
B. & Mortg. $65,000 $178,205
N.Y. 5 pr cts 113,205   The amount which may be rea-
lized from a forced sale of the bonds and mortgages, is so
very problematical, that we should guess that the Controller will be able to pay 80 cents on the dollar for the notes.

NORTHERN EXCHANGE BANK.
Securities.   Circulation.
New-York 5's. $65,000 $65,000

BANK of CAYUGA LAKE.
New-York 5's, $50,000 $50,000

STATE BANK, SAUGERTIES.
New-York 5's, $50,000 $50,000
As New-York stocks are now selling, the notes of the
three last named banks are worth from 90 to 92 cents on
the dollar.

DELAWARE BRIDGE.
It is not in our power to advise, understandingly, in re-
lation to this Bank—we do not believe it will be resuscitated.
For the present, we are paying 30 cents on the dollar. It
may be be better, an l it may be worse.

SUSQUEHANNA COUNTY BANK.
We are paying 60 cents on the dollar for the notes of
this bank, and there appears to be some demand for them.

Counterfeit Gold Pieces.

A quarter eagle, purporting to be of the New-
Orleans mint, of 1843, after being pronounced
genuine by the best judges in Wall-street, was
sent to the Philadelphia mint, where it under-
went all the ordinary tests, and compared with
a genuine piece of the N. O. mint, under a pow-
erful microscope, but no difference could be seen,
except that the edge was slightly more rounded,
which might have been occasioned by wear.—
Upon being sawn in two, it proved to be only a
shell of gold, over a filling of silver. The gold
was worth $1,25. Half eagles, of the same
character, have been discovered. Eagles are so
depreciated by *sweating*, as to be worth but $9.

Counterfeit Treasury Notes.

The public are cautioned against spurious Treasury
Notes. A $500 note, sent to this city, from Nashville, had
been altered from a note engraved in New-Orleans, for the
Eagle Mining Company of Indiana, having for a vignette
a stooping eagle on the limb of a tree, with Washington on
the left end, and the goddess of Commerce on the right.—
The above description will enable any person to detect this
fraud, as it differs in all the particulars from the genuine
Treasury Notes.

To the Mercantile Community.

Merchants wishing to send their Cards or Business Cir-
culars to their friends in the country, can occupy the first
page of this paper, and have any number of the *Reporter*,
at the following rates:—

1,000 copies......$25,00   250 copies......$8,00
500 copies...... 15,00   100 copies...... 5,00

THOMPSON'S
BANK NOTE REPORTER
AND
COIN CHART MANUAL.

PUBLISHED AND CORRECTED BY

J. THOMPSON, STOCK and EXCHANGE BROKER,
No. 64 Wall Street, New-York.

The *Reporter* is published daily, (Sundays
excepted,) and furnished to subscribers, weekly,
semi-monthly, or monthly, as may be ordered.

A paper like the *Reporter*, is an indispensable
assistant to every business man : to large dealers
it is useful as a reference for the current rates of
discount, with valuable tables (to be found from
time to time on the first and last pages—always
brief and comprehensive,) on banking and mone-
tary affairs in general, with hints on the above,
useful to all. To the smaller dealers, it is a
great aid in judging of bills, discriminating between the spurious and genuine; and in this way,
in many cases, saving *ten times* the price of sub-
scription, every year.

TERMS: Weekly.......$2,00 per year.
Semi-monthly,. 1,00 " In advance.
Monthly....... 50 cts "

All *regular subscribers* are entitled to a copy
of our GOLD and SILVER COIN SHEET,
containing a *larger number* of fac-similes of the
foreign coins in circulation, *than ever published* in
any one collection. This sheet will be improved
by the 1st of July next, and *all* our subscribers
furnished with a copy, free of expense.

Newspaper agents and dealers generally, can
be supplied with the Reporter and coins attached,
if so ordered. Address,

J. THOMPSON,
Stock & Exchange Broker, 64 Wall st., N.Y.

Extracts from from the Controller's Report for 1848.

"In the cases of five hooks, the right of the Controller to
sell certain mortgages was called in question at the auction,
and in those cases the mortgages were withdrawn from the
sole and foreclosed in chancery. The first of these was a
mortgage of $4,275, pledged for the notes of the Bank of
America, at Buffalo.—The litigation in this case is not yet
close l. Another was a mortgage of $10,000, given to se-
cure the redemption of the notes of the Merchants Exch. Bk,
of Buffalo. In the case of the Farmers Bank, of Seneca
county, there were two mortgages contested. There is a
mortgage of $2,500 pledged for the notes of the Bank of
Brockport, also in the course of collection. The Washington Bank, of New-York, had deposited with the Controller
a mortgage of $10,000 which was contested."

May not the same difficulty arise in closing up the Atlas
and James' Banks?

In commenting on the 1st class of free banks, the Controller says :

"In almost every case the notes of these Banks are secured by stocks of the state of New-York ; so that the notes
would be half a per cent better after the death of a bank
than during its life."

We want it pretty strong for the "1st class," but this
beats us a feet.

The Banks.

                           Failed.   Selling at.
New Hope Delaware Bridge,..Dec. 27, at 10 a.m...40 cents
Susquehannah County,........Dec. 28, at 10 a.m...60 cents
Atlas Bank of Clymer,........Dec. 27, at 12 noon, 75 cents
James Bank of Janesville,...Dec. 30, at 12 noon, 70 cents
Northern Exchange Bank,....Jan. 10, at 12 noon, 85 cents
Bank of Cayuga Lake,........Jan. 19, at 2 p.m. 83 cents
State Bank at Saugerties,....Jan. 19, at 2 p.m. 85 cents
Lewistown Bank, Pa........November,   cents

These are all the banks which have failed during the
pressure and panic.

Lightning Source UK Ltd.
Milton Keynes UK
UKHW012159150219
337363UK00004B/158/P